Slow Cooker Cookbook

Chef Approved Slow Cooker Recipes Made For Your Slow Cooker – Cook More Eat Better

Table of Contents

Introduction

Slow Cookers became famous when the Rival Company introduced the crock-pot back in 1971. Right after their introduction, Slow Cookers became the favorite cooking utensil of every working family. Slow Cooker companies have continued to expand their range in the last 20 years, and they are now an inseparable part of every American household.

In a world where people have to work all the time, it can be a little tiring to come home and cook. Even if you do decide to cook, there's a pretty good chance that you will be too tired to make something delicious and healthy. This is where the Slow Cooker comes in – it's an ideal solution for all of your cooking problems. All you have to do is throw the ingredients into the Slow Cooker, and you'll come back to a perfectly cooked meal that your whole family can enjoy.

Slow Cookers are perfect for everyone; they can cater to a single person, roommates, partners and even a whole family. You won't have to tire yourself by sitting in the kitchen for hours and, with just a little bit of effort, you'll get a beautifully cooked meal.

Now, many people continue to think that Slow Cookers can only be used to cook a few types of food. This book has been written to dispel that myth; slow cookers can cook any kind of food, from lasagna to nutritional gourmet meals. In this book, you'll find a list of recipes that will allow you to maximize the potential of your slow cooker. You will also learn about the basics of slow cooking, its history and even the features of a slow cooker.

Thank you for buying this book!

Chapter 1: What is a Slow Cooker?

When you have a busy schedule, a deadline approaching at work or your kid's school project to complete, how will you find time to prepare a healthy meal? This is where the slow cooker comes in.

You will be able to make nutritious meals using the slow cooker. You will initially be surprised at how easy it is to cook with a slow cooker, and will then probably begin to wonder why you had not changed over earlier. After all of that, you will be able to focus on cooking these meals that are delicious and healthy too.

Do you know what the best part of this slow cooker is? You will be able to save time and also make nutritious meals for your family, but the greatest part about this is that you will finally be able to lose the excess weight that you have been trying so hard to lose. You will never have to spend hours in the kitchen when you use a slow cooker. That's is the beauty of a slow cooker it comes with a timer based cooking mechanism, where the food cooks for hours over low heat, while you get on with your usual life. Yes, a slow cooker will cook your food while you go about your work and will turn off on its own when the food is cooked.

A unique cooking method that feels like cheating, slow cooking offers an excellent way to cook. Whether you and your roommate have different schedules or you and your spouse work different shifts, everyone can come home to a delicious, nutritious, home-cooked meal that's ready to eat. Plus, slow cooking is a money saver as it turns those tough, less expensive cuts of meat into melt-in-your-mouth revelations after long cooking in a low, moist heat.

If meat is not your thing, you can make plenty of other dishes in your slow cooker — from breakfast to beans to casseroles and more. Slow cooking recipes have come a long way since the introduction of the appliance. Gone are the bland recipes that use minimal herbs and spices and end up looking just about as appetizing as the plate they're on. With this cookbook, you can choose to have all kinds of delicious meals.

Slow cookers are cheap, easy to use and very economical. They offer a healthier alternative to other modern means of cooking like ovens and microwaves. Slow cookers are all about cooking food in a more tasty way. It also adds a lot of flavor to the food since it's cooked under extreme pressure and in a closed environment.

Most people know that slow cookers are ideal appliances for making big batches of food. But, depending on the size you buy, slow cookers can also be perfect for making meals for two or three. Slow cooking is so much easier and healthier than cooking a microwave dinner or going to a drive-through for some fast food, and the food that comes out of this appliance is delicious, well flavored, complex and interesting. One of the best benefits of the slow cooker is the aroma when you open the front door!

Components

There are three main elements in a slow cooker: an outer casing, an inner container and a lid.

The external/outer casing is metal and contains low-wattage warming coils, the segment in charge of cooking the food, and the external casing embodies these warming coils. The internal compartment, which is additionally called a crock, is made of coated clay and fits inside the metal warming component. In a few models, you can expel this cooking container from the external shell. The third bit of the machine is a domed top that fits firmly onto the vessel.

The apparatus cooks based on a blend of wattage and time. At the point when turned on, the electrical coils warm up and exchanges heart in a roundabout way from the external packaging to the space between the base divider and the stoneware compartment. This circuitous warmth heats the vessel to the vicinity of 180 and 300 degrees Fahrenheit (82 to 149 degrees Celsius). This strategy for heat exchange stews the ingredients inside the container at a low temperature for a few hours, until the food is completely cooked.

As the meal cooks, it discharges steam, which the top traps. The buildup makes a vacuum seal between the top and the edge of the container, which adds dampness to the ingredients while helping the cooking procedure - the cover is essential to the cooking method. The moderate cooker has three settings: low, high and off. In programmable cookers, the gadget will change to a warm setting after it has cooked the meal to keep the food at an appropriate temperature.

Difference between Slow Cooker and Crock-Pot

There is a lot of confusion about what the difference is between a Slow Cooker and a crock-pot. Many people use both the terms interchangeably without realizing that it is wrong.

Slow cooker is the generic name for an appliance that has heating elements all around the insert that quickly brings food up to safe temperatures. Crock-pot is the Rival

Corporation's registered trademark for its slow cookers. In simple words, every crock-pot is a slow cooker, but every slow cooker is not a crock-pot. Other popular slow cooker brands include All Clad, Cuisinart and Hamilton Beach.

Slow Cooker 101

How it Works

A true slow cooker consists of a thin round or oval metal surround encasing a metal or ceramic insert. A glass or plastic lid fits snugly onto the insert. Heating coils in the surround heat up and evenly heat the insert, which then transfers heat to the food.

Temperature

Most slow cookers come with three settings: keep warm, low, and high. The keep-warm temperature is about 160° F, just above the lowest safe temperature (140 ° F) for holding food. Low is about 200° F, and high is about 300° F. Most of the recipes use the low setting so that you can cook for at least seven hours, giving you an entire day, or night, to walk away from the slow cooker. The general rule of thumb is that one hour on high is equal to two hours on low.

Steam Cooking

Because the lid fits snugly, steam gets trapped in the slow cooker as the food heats up. This "wet" cooking method cooks gently and thoroughly. The steam also creates a slight vacuum seal between the lid and the insert, which keeps volatile nutrients such as vitamins B and C in the slow cooker while locking in flavor compounds. Wet cooking methods are excellent with tougher cuts of meat, soups, stews, casseroles and side dishes.

Myths

1. Slow Cooked Food is Bland - Long, slow cooking using wet heat can mute the flavors of herbs, but that is easily fixed by adding more of the herbs just before serving. Slow cooked foods are more flavorful than foods cooked on the stovetop since there is no evaporation of volatile compounds.
2. Slow Cookers are only good for certain kind of foods - Your slow cooker can make lasagna, mashed potatoes, beans, grains, breakfast cereals, bread puddings and even cheesecakes.
3. Slow Cookers overcook vegetables - The key to cooking perfectly tender vegetables is layering. Tough root vegetables should be prepped into even cuts and placed at the bottom. More tender veggies such as corn and peas should be at the top.

4. Slow Cooked food is watery and thin - Do not add more liquid to your slow cooker than the recipe specifies. There is no evaporation during cooking, and the ingredients give off liquid as they cook.
5. Slow cookers don't cook food evenly - Again, layering is essential for even cooking. Tough vegetables belong at the bottom; followed by meats, then tender vegetables on top. And make sure vegetables and fruits with the same texture are cut to the same size, so they cook evenly.

Do's and Don't

There are some rules you must follow when using a slow cooker, both for safety and ensure that the finished result will be delicious.

Do's

1. Spray the Insert with Nonstick Cooking Spray before Adding Food - The food will not stick to the insert, and cleanup will be much easier.
2. Think about Sautéing Aromatics such as Onions and Garlic before you add them - Doing so helps the flavor develop and these vegetables will become sweet and tender.
3. Thaw Frozen food before adding them to the Slow Cooker - Frozen foods may stay in the danger zone of 40 ° F to 140 ° F too long and will reduce the temperature of other foods as they cook. Substantial frozen foods, such as pot roast, may not cook through in the allotted time. Thaw these foods overnight in the refrigerator— never on the counter.
4. Cut the Same Densities of Food into the Same Size Pieces - Carrots, potatoes, onions, and sweet potatoes should be the same size, so they cook evenly and at the same time.
5. Use Wooden, Plastic, or Nonstick Utensils when stirring or Serving Food - Metal tools can scratch the ceramic insert, causing liquid to seep out and the insert to eventually crack.

Don't:

- Lift the lid to Check on the Food as the Slow Cooker is cooking - Every time you lift the lid, the steam and the slight vacuum seal between the lid and insert is released. Hence, dropping the temperature and lengthening the cooking time.
- Add too much Liquid - There is little to no evaporation in a slow cooker. Adding more liquid than the recipe calls for will result in soggy food that has little flavor.

- Store Food in the Insert - The insert is made for holding heat. If you store hot food in the insert and keep it in the refrigerator, the food will take too long to cool to a safe temperature and bacteria may grow.
- Add Ground Meats without pre-cooking them - Ground meats will become mushy and fatty if put in the slow cooker uncooked, ultimately this adds too much fat to the recipe.
- Add Ingredients such as Pasta, Shrimp, Tender Vegetables, or Dairy before the last 30 Minutes of Cooking Time - Pasta, shrimp and tender veggies can easily overcook, and dairy will curdle if heated too long.

Chapter 2: Slow Cooking History

The story of the slow cooker started from the Naxon Utilities Corporation situated in Chicago. The company worked under the leadership and guidance of Irving Naxon, and he was the person who developed the Naxon Beanery All-Purpose Cooker. Naxon later stated that the inspiration that he got for creating it was a story from his Jewish grandmother about cooking when she used to live in a small Lithuanian town with her family. She talked about how her mother used to make a stew called cholent, and it took many hours to cook, that too in an oven.

An advertisement from the 1950s shows something called a "Simmer Crock" which was under the ownership of the Industrial Radiant Heat Corp, a company from Gladstone, NJ. The Rival Company stepped into the business by buying Naxon in 1970. They then introduced the product as the slow cooker in 1971.

Soon after the Rival Company launched the first slow cooker, called the Slow Cooker, in 1971, most slow-cooker recipes consisted of some meat, cream of "something" soup, and a few vegetables that cooked into a hearty, but boring "hot dish." It was such a novelty to throw food into an appliance, turn it on, leave the house, and come home to a finished dinner. Working mothers, in particular, embraced this new trend. Since the slow-cooker recipes at the time focused more on convenience than taste, it wasn't long before the complaints started to trickle in. Many thought the food was under-flavored, that everything that came out of it looked the same, or that the recipes relied too much on canned and processed foods.

In 1974, the Rival Company tried to solve the problem of cleaning by introducing removable stoneware. By the early 1980s, interest in the slow cooker had waned.

About fifteen years ago, new versions of the slow cooker started appearing on the market. Chefs started inventing slow-cooker recipes that made the slow cooker's old reputation recede— recipes like Cuban black beans and rice, French Cassoulet, or spicy tamales. A slowing economy and more women in the workforce meant more people were looking for ways to prepare delicious food quickly that would still fit within the family budget. The slow cooker seemed the ideal solution.

Presently, the brand is under Sunbeam Products, which is a subsidiary of Jarden Corporation. Other brands currently sell this appliance – GE, Cuisinart, Hamilton Beach, Magic Chef, Kitchen Aid, West Bend Housewares, and the American Electric Corporation, which is now defunct.

Chapter 3: Different Features and Functions of Common Slow Cookers

Slow cookers come in a wide variety of features ranging from different shapes and patterns to transportability (great if you're doing a potluck) to programmable timing. You'll find that most 3-quart slow cookers on the market these days are round while the 3 ½-quart models are rectangular, oval, or round. They are available in fun patterns and colors from flowers to tiger stripes and stainless to magenta. Make sure your slow cooker has a removable insert for easier cleaning. Luckily, most of the slow cookers on the market today have this feature.

It's important to be aware of the different features and functions that slow cookers come with if you want to cook well. This will also help you to select the best slow cooker for your home.

This chapter will tell you about the different features in Slow Cookers and which one you should pick for the best results.

Size

You may already own a slow cooker that you want to use today, but the size of the slow cooker must be appropriate for the recipe amounts. To cook safely, slow cookers must be filled one-half to three-quarters full. The best sizes of slow cooker are also the most common: 3- or 3 ½-quart slow cookers. You can find them in most big-box stores as well as online but be careful about the quality of the place you are buying from. These slow cookers will hold about 7 to 9 cups of food to serve two people generously, with the possibility of leftovers for lunch the next day. So if you make lasagna in a slow cooker this size, you can enjoy it for dinner and have enough left over for a ready-made lunch the next day— but you won't be stuck eating it the entire week. None of these recipes will require making space in your freezer, except for broths and sauces made in bulk and side dishes.

Temperature

Slow cookers still have two temperatures - the low-heat setting and the high-heat setting— but the keep-warm feature is relatively new. The ability to program cooking time is precious if you are gone for more than eight hours during the day. With this feature, once the slow cooker gets to the end of the cook time, it doesn't just turn off but switches over to the keep-warm setting for two hours. Don't forget that new slow cookers cook at hotter temperatures than those made ten years ago. Back then the low setting was 180 ° F (today it's about 200 ° F), and the high setting was 230 ° F (today it's about 300 ° F). So if you are using an older slow cooker, you may need to increase the time the food cooks when you make these recipes.

When you're shopping, keep in mind that there are appliances on the market referred to as slow cookers that have their heating element only on the bottom. Appliances with heating elements only on the bottom heat food more slowly. Experts do not recommend cooking large cuts of meat in this type of slow cooker (although it works for soups and stews). When purchasing your slow cooker, make sure it is a true one— with heating elements all around the insert.

Brand

Slow cookers, you will find, are a relatively inexpensive investment with many brands to choose from. Rival makes the most popular brand, crock-pot. Their 3-quart color crock-pot and stainless steel crock-pot sells for about $20. The 3 ½-quart model is available for about $40 in a rectangular shape, which is perfect for making dishes such as lasagna. Rival also makes a 3 ½-quart oval crock-pot that will hook up to other slow cookers for buffet serving. Those are more expensive, at around $50.

Hamilton Beach makes a lot of pretty 3-quart slow cookers that come with a metal surround in different colors and patterns. The prices for these slow cookers range from $25 to $40, depending on the design. The slow cookers have warm, low, and high settings.

Cuisinart has a programmable 3½-quart slow cooker that makes slow cooking about as easy as you can imagine. The oval shape and stainless steel surround are very attractive, and the cooker has to keep warm, simmer, low, and high settings. It sells for about $60.

Heating Method

Every slow cooker has an inner pot that is removable and one which can be used to serve food. Certain brands have this part made from an aluminum cast, which makes it easier to sear different kinds of meat in the slow cooker itself. You will not have to use a stove to sear the meat. But, the thing to remember is that aluminum is not a very safe metal to use to cook since the temperatures increase inside the pot. The important thing to remember is that a slow cooker is based on cooking with low heat.

Sometimes the element that provides heat can be at the bottom, and if you have some good luck, then the element might even go up the side of the base – this allows for the heat to be distributed evenly throughout the cooker.

There are slow cookers in the market that come with a crock that is on top of the unit, which provides heating. Heat does not get equally distributed this way, and you will be forced to constantly stir the food to ensure perfect cooking. This is obviously not possible because this is opposite to the principle of a slow cooker, which allows a person to leave the food to cook instead of watching it all the time. So, be careful when you're buying a slow cooker and check what kind of heating method comes with it.

It's also important to buy a slow cooker whose heating method you understand. It is important to realize how fast your slow cooker heats the food – which is dependent on the number of heating units. If you are not aware of this while cooking, then you might overcook or even burn the food.

Faster Cooking

Slow cookers can work without any supervision and prepare food for close to eight hours. Some slow cookers can allow you to prepare these meals within a few hours without having to wait for too long. But, it is always good to avoid making food this way since a slow cooker is all about cooking slowly to preserve the nutrition.

You need to remember to learn how to use a slow cooker irrespective of how many settings may be available in this appliance.

Chapter 4: Slow Cooking Tips

This chapter will list some general and specific tips that you can apply when you are slow cooking. These tips will help you use your slow cooker more efficiently, and you will also learn about how you can develop your meals to be tastier and healthier.

General Tips

- If you are a little skeptical of preparing meals in the slow cooker when you are away from home, you can easily find different meals to substitute. You can cook meals overnight and not worry about burning the house down since this electric appliance is user-friendly and will turn off the minute the food has cooked thoroughly.
- When you need to clean the slow cooker, you will need to just rub the inside of the slow cooker with oil or a cooking spray that will not stick to the insides. It is always easy to clean the liners of the slow cooker, but you will need to make sure that you do it often to avoid messing the slow cooker up.
- Before you cook any frozen poultry or meat, you will need to bring them down to room temperature to ensure that the meat is cooked through fully. You can brown them on a stovetop before you put them inside the cooker.
- Always make sure that you only fill two-thirds of the cooker. You need to remember that if you cook too little and too much in the slow cooker, you will be affecting the cooking time and the quality of the food.
- Since the vegetables usually take longer to cook when compared to meat and other poultry, you should cook them first. Place the meat in the slow cooker over the vegetables and top them with broth, sauce or water.
- You will need to add the broth, barbecue sauce or water to the slow cooker depending on the recipe you are using. Since the sauces take longer to reduce, you can cook them for longer in the slow cooker to reduce.
- If you find it easier, you can set the slow cooker on high for the first one hour and then turn the heat lower to finish cooking.
- Always keep the lid of the slow cooker in place when you are cooking. If you keep moving the lid of the slow cooker, you will be losing out on the cooking time.
- Always add the pasta and other grains to the slow cooker only in the end to avoid having a mushy dish. The other option could be to cook pasta and grains separately and only add them to the dish before you serve.

- Always add cream and milk only in the last half an hour to avoid the curdling of these dairy products.
- When it comes to soft vegetables, you can add them only during the last half an hour of the cooking process.
- Always check up on your dish when half the cooking time is done. You do not necessarily have to, but it is good to do this.

Converting a Stove-Top

One of the best things about the slow cooker is that you can take a stovetop recipe and adjust a few details to make it work in the appliance. Soups, chilies, stews, roasts and meat with vegetables are all perfect for conversion.

Keep these principles in mind:

1. Decrease the amount of liquid called for by about half. But keep in mind this caveat: For any recipe that cooks rice, pasta, or beans, you must have twice as much liquid as ingredient by weight to cook properly, since they absorb water as they cook. So, for example, a recipe that uses one cup of rice should have at least two cups of liquid.
2. Trim excess fat from meats and poultry. Too much fat in a slow cooker will raise the temperature, and the food may overcook. Plus, excess fat will make the food unpleasantly greasy.
3. Put veggies in the bottom and meats on top for even cooking. Although everything cooks together in a saucepan or pot on the stove, proper layering is essential to avoid overcooking vegetables in the slow cooker.

In general, 1 hour of simmering on the stovetop is equal to 6 to 8 hours on low in the slow cooker. A recipe that simmers for 30 minutes would cook in 4 to 6 hours on low in the slow cooker.

Using Foil

You definitely want to have heavy-duty aluminum foil on hand if you plan to use your slow cooker often. Foil is a versatile tool with many uses.

Make slings out of the foil to put under meatloaf or lasagna so you can lift the finished product right out of the appliance. Tear off a 24-inch piece of heavy-duty foil, and fold it in half lengthwise two or three times. Place it in the slow cooker. Repeat with the second piece of foil, and then place this piece in the slow cooker so the foil crosses, making an "X" at the bottom.

Line the slow cooker with foil for super-easy cleanup and to shield the edges to prevent overcooking or burning. Pasta dishes and casseroles do well with a foil liner.

Layer vegetables, meat, seasonings and a bit of liquid on a piece of heavy-duty foil to make individual one-dish meals. Close the packets and place them in the slow cooker.

Ball up pieces of aluminum foil to roast a chicken in the slow cooker. The extra height acts like a rack, keeping the bird out of the rendered liquid so that it roasts instead of braises.

Shopping for Meals

Shopping can sometimes feel like a juggling act. You need to limit the amount you buy so you don't waste food, but packages are often geared toward excessive meals. Your hands aren't entirely tied, however. With a few targeted tips, you'll have no problem keeping any waste to a minimum.

Fresh Produce, Meat and Herbs

If possible, purchase the fresh foods that you store in the refrigerator a few times a week so that your recipes use the freshest possible ingredients. Planning your menu weekly helps decrease the chance of any food going to waste. During your planning, determine whether you can use ingredients more than once. For instance, if you need ¼ cup of chopped bell pepper for one recipe, pick another recipe that will use the rest of the vegetable later in the week. Be sure to store cut produce in plastic bags so they don't wilt or dry out. You can also add any leftover vegetables to other recipes, even if they aren't called for. For example, chopped zucchini would be a great addition to chicken soup or even chili, and leftover green beans would be delicious added to a pot roast.

Storage Items

Purchase foods that keep well in the pantry in bulk, and make sure you compare the price per ounce of different-size packages. For instance, if you cook with dried beans often, a 5-pound bag, which will last for at least a year, is a better buy than a 16-ounce bag. Canned foods will last for years and should be consistently replenished. When it comes to dried spices, however, buy small bottles, as these lose their strength after a year.

Animal Protein

Make sure you carefully check expiration dates on meat, seafood, and poultry so you know you're preparing food that is safe to eat. Don't buy more meat than a recipe calls for unless you are prepared to repackage and freeze some of it.

Fresh Produce

Purchase just enough tender produce, like bell peppers or tomatoes, for a specific recipe. This is where menu planning goes a long way toward helping you buy just what you need, and no more. Harder fare, like onions, potatoes, sweet potatoes, and garlic, can be purchased in larger quantities, but be careful how you store them. Onions and potatoes should be stored away from each other, since keeping them in proximity can cause the other to spoil rapidly.

Herbs

Purchase fresh herbs in small quantities as well. To keep them fresh longer, cut off the ends and store them upright in a small glass of water in the fridge. To store fresh herbs longer, chop them up, place in a small container in 1-tbsp amounts, and freeze. Frozen herbs can be added directly to the slow cooker without thawing first.

Cooking with Different Meats

What part of the animal gets you the tastiest dinner?

The chicken parts to use are bone-in chicken breasts and boneless thighs. With the breasts, the bone slows down the chicken's rate of cooking and adds lots of flavor to the entire dish. A bone-in chicken breast will cook in 6 to 7 hours, while a boneless one cooks in 4 to 5 hours. Don't forget to remove the skin— it becomes flabby with this cooking method— and don't brown the chicken before cooking unless the recipe calls for it.

The best beef cuts for the slow cooker include chuck eye roast, flank steak, bottom round, brisket, and short ribs. These inexpensive cuts become very tender when cooked in moist heat at low temperatures. Be sure to trim off excess fat before cooking these cuts. You can brown them before cooking in the slow cooker to add flavor, but that step isn't necessary, with the exception of ground beef, which must be browned and drained before use in slow-cooker recipes.

All types of pork work well in the slow cooker, from boneless chops to loin roasts. Chops become meltingly tender, while pork shoulder can be shredded into a tender tangle that is perfect for sandwiches. Again, remember to trim and discard excess fat from pork cuts.

Chapter 5: Benefits and Advantages

Benefits

You may have heard a lot of people tell you about how great a slow cooker is but may never have considered purchasing one. When you own a slow cooker of a good brand, you will find all your cooking fantasies come true. You would not have to stand in front of a hot stove and cook for hours after a long day of work. Imagine how great it would be if you came into the house to the smell of a slowly cooked chicken or herb cooked salmon? That will definitely be heaven would it not? You will be able to cook meals that are nutritious and healthy and would also be able to spend lesser time in front of the stove.

After having read all this, you may probably be under the impression that you will not have to do anything. But, there is some prep that you will need to do in order to have a lot of healthy and nutritious meals. You may need to brown the meat on the stovetop and may need to chop and dice your vegetables before you put them inside the slow cooker. Once all the prep is done, you will just need to put all the vegetables and the other ingredients into the slow cooker and just go about your day. You will come back home to a well-prepared meal.

The best part about a slow cooker is that the meal will be ready in no time and if it is ready faster than you anticipated, you will find that the pot has moved to the warm mode and has preserved your food the way it should be. Let's take a look at a few more benefits of cooking with a slow cooker.

Delicious and Nutritious meals

The ingredients are all fresh and cooked at low temperatures for a longer period of time. Since the vegetables and other ingredients are all cooked slowly, and are not subjected to too much heat, the nutrients will be preserved in these ingredients. All the juices in the vegetables will also remain intact, which would make the food more succulent and delicious.

Saves time

When you cook using a stovetop, you will be spending hours to ensure that the ingredients you are using are cooked to perfection. But, when it comes to a slow cooker, you will not have to worry since you will only need to do the initial prep. Your slow cooker will take care of everything else for you. You can go about doing what you would normally do.

Always useful

You will never have to worry about when you can use a slow cooker to make meals since they are season friendly. You can use these appliances any time of the year! The advantage of a slow cooker is that it eliminates the need to use an oven and also prevents your house from heating up too much.

Lesser Energy Consumption

You will find that a slow cooker uses substantially lesser amounts of energy when compared with an electric oven.

Very Easy to Clean

You will only need to clean up the cutting board, a knife and maybe the pan that you have used to brown the meat you will be cooking. Apart from that you will only need to clean the slow cooker as opposed to cleaning multiple utensils.

Portable

A slow cooker is easy to transfer. You will not have the need to transfer the meal onto a serving plate if you do not want to.

When you shop for a slow cooker, you will have to always factor in the number of people you will be cooking for. You will be able to prepare lovely meals using a slow cooker. You need to remember to care for your slow cooker too. Let us take a look at a few tips that will come in handy when you are using a slow cooker to make your meals.

Advantages

You might be wondering why you should cook with a slow cooker instead of your traditional cooking methods. This chapter will list all the advantages that a Slow Cooker has over any other cooking method.

Slow cookers are unique appliances, different from a stand-alone roaster or steamer. Here are a handful of reasons slow cooking just makes sense:

Healthier than other cooking methods

Slow cooking is a healthy way to cook food. The low temperatures cook food safely but slowly, preserving valuable nutrients. When food is cooked at high heat, harmful compounds such as advanced glycation end products (AGEs) form. AGEs contribute to insulin resistance and inflammation. The slow cooker completely eliminates this risk. Also, using fresh foods and avoiding highly processed ingredients is a much healthier choice than other timesaving alternatives such as prepackaged meals and frozen dinners.

Frees up time

You'll save lots of time in the kitchen when you use a slow cooker. Most of these recipes involve just a few preparation steps; then you combine everything in the appliance and turn it on.

Saves you money

You can use much less expensive cuts of meat in the slow cooker. Expensive beef cuts such as filet mignon do not cook well in low, moist heat. Cuts such as chuck and round are perfect for the slow cooker's self-basting mechanism. Less expensive chicken thighs also cook to tender perfection in the slow cooker. Cheaper root vegetables such as turnips, potatoes, and carrots are also ideal ingredients for this cooking method.

Delicious Results

Meat becomes incredibly tender in this appliance. Connective tissue and gelatin break down in beef, pork, lamb, and poultry when cooked in the slow cooker, and the fat melts and spreads through the cut. Vegetables, especially hard root vegetables, become fork tender and very sweet. Grains, including oatmeal, Farro, wild rice and barley, cook to nutty and tender perfection. You can even make amazing desserts, from rich puddings to decadent cakes.

Eco-friendly cooking

Your slow cooker is a great energy saver. It will not heat up the kitchen in the summer and put a strain on your air conditioner. A slow cooker will use about 125 watts per hour on low. That works out to about 1.5 cents per hour in an area that charges 12 cents per kilowatt-hour. The average oven costs about 10 cents per kilowatt-hour, so even with a shorter cooking time, using your oven costs more.

Chapter 6: Slow Cooker Breakfast Recipes

Apple Pie Oats

Ingredients:

- 2 apples, peeled, cored, diced
- 1 cup steel cut oats
- 2 cups coconut milk
- 1 tbsp. brown sugar or to taste
- 1 tsp. cinnamon
- 1 cup water
- 1 tbsp. coconut oil
- ½ tsp. salt or to taste

Method:

1. Spray oil inside the slow cooker thoroughly.
2. Add all the ingredients in the slow cooker.
3. Set on Low and cook for 5-7 hours. (You can do a trial sometime during the take to see how long it takes to cook)
4. Serve with topping of your choice.

Berry Muffins

Ingredients:

- 2 eggs
- 4 cups all-purpose flour
- 1 1/2 cups whole milk
- 1 1/2 cups raspberries
- 1 1/2 cups blueberries
- 1 1/2 cups granulated sugar
- 1 cup unsalted butter, melted
- 1 cup mini semi-sweet chocolate chips
- 4 tsp. baking powder
- 1/2 tsp. salt
- 1/2 tsp. vanilla extract

Method:

- Place the berries in a bowl and add about 1/2 cup flour over it and toss to coat the berries with flour and aside.
- Whisk together eggs, milk and vanilla in a bowl and set aside.
- Add remaining flour to a large bowl along with 1-cup sugar, baking powder and salt. Add butter and mix well.
- Pour the egg mixture into the flour mixture and mix well (you may find that the batter is not smooth and may have some lumps
- Add chocolate chips and berry mixture and fold gently. Pour batter into lined or greased muffin molds (up to 3/4). Cook them in batches if necessary.
- Pour 6 ounces water into the slow cooker. Place an aluminum foil at the bottom of the cooker. Place the muffin molds inside the cooker. Sprinkle the remaining sugar over the batter in the muffin molds.
- Cover and set the cooker on High for 2 1/2 - 3 hour. Insert a toothpick at the center of each muffin. If it comes out clean, then the muffins are ready else cook for another 20-30 minutes.
- Let it cool completely in the cooker. Loosen the edges and invert on to plates and serve.

Slow Cooked Breakfast Casserole

Ingredients:

- 6 ounce pork sausage roll
- ½ cup cheese of your choice
- ½ cup low fat milk
- ½ tsp. coriander powder
- ½ tsp. garlic powder
- ½ tsp. chili powder
- ½ tsp. cumin powder
- Salt and pepper to taste
- Avocado (optional)
- Sour cream (optional)
- Salsa (optional)

Method:

1. Place a skillet over medium heat. Add the sausage. Cook for a few minutes until it is no longer pink.
2. Add salsa salt, pepper, chili powder, and cumin and coriander powders. Mix well and remove from heat.
3. Whisk together eggs and milk in a large bowl. Add the pork and cheese. Mix well.
4. Transfer into a greased slow cooker.
5. Cover the pot and cook on low for 5 hours or on high for 2 ½ hours.
6. Serve with toppings if desired.

Egg and Broccoli Casserole

Ingredients:

- 5 oz. frozen broccoli, thawed and drained
- 3/4 cup beaten egg
- 1 1/2 tbsp. finely chopped onion
- 1/6 cup flour
- 12 oz. cottage cheese
- 1/8 cup melted unsalted butter
- 1 1/4 cups shredded Cheddar cheese, divided

Method:

1. Lightly grease the slow cooker with cooking oil.
2. Mix together the egg, cottage cheese, butter, onion, flour, 1 cup of cheddar cheese, and broccoli in the slow cooker.
3. Cover the slow cooker and cook for 1 hour on high, then stir up the ingredients and put the heat to low.
4. Cover and cook for 2 hours and 30 minutes, then top with the rest of the cheddar cheese. Serve warm.

Slow Cooked Nutella French toast

Ingredients:

- ½ loaf challah bread, cut into cubes
- 3 large eggs
- 2 bananas, sliced
- 1 cup vanilla flavored almond milk
- 1 tsp. vanilla extract
- 2 tbsp. Nutella + extra for topping
- ½ tsp. ground cinnamon
- A pinch salt
- ½ tbsp. unsalted butter
- ½ tbsp. brown sugar

Method:

1. Place the bread cubes in the slow cooker.
2. Whisk together eggs, milk, cinnamon, vanilla, salt and Nutella in a bowl and transfer it into the slow cooker over the bread cubes. Mix well.
3. Cover and cook on High for 2 hours or on Low for 4 hours. If possible stir in between.
4. Meanwhile, place a nonstick pan over medium high heat. Add butter.
5. When butter melts, add banana and brown sugar and mix well. Cook until the bananas are light brown on both the sides.
6. To serve: Place some Nutella mixture over individual serving plates. Place a little of the bananas over it.
7. Top with some Nutella and serve.

Cauliflower and Sausage Casserole

Ingredients:

- 1 medium head cauliflower, shredded
- 6 eggs
- 5 ounce package cooked sausages, sliced
- ¼ cup milk
- 1 cup cheddar cheese, shredded
- ½ tsp. dry mustard
- 1 small onion, chopped
- Salt to taste
- Pepper powder to taste
- Cooking spray

Method:

1. Spray the slow cooker pot with cooking spray.
2. In a bowl, add eggs, milk, mustard, salt and pepper. Whisk well.
3. Place half the cauliflower at the bottom of the pot. Spread well. Next sprinkle half the onions. Sprinkle salt and pepper. Lay half the sausages and half the cheese over the sausages.
4. Repeat step 3 with the remaining half ingredients.
5. Pour the beaten egg mixture all over the cooker pot.
6. Cover and cook on low for 5-7 hours or until the top is golden brown.

Carrot Zucchini Oatmeal

Ingredients:

- 1 cup steel cut oats
- 1 large carrot, peeled, grated
- 1 small zucchini, peeled, grated
- 1/2 cup pecans, chopped
- 1/8 tsp. ground nutmeg
- 1/8 tsp. ground cloves
- 3/4 tsp. ground cinnamon
- 3 cups vanilla flavored milk
- 2 tsp. vanilla extract
- 4 tbsp. agave nectar or maple syrup

Method:

1. Add all the ingredients except pecans to the slow cooker at night and stir.
2. Cover and set on Low for 8 hours or on High for 4 hours.
3. Add pecans before serving. You can add more milk if you desire.

Chapter 7: Slow Cooker Brunch Recipes

Apple and Cherry Risotto

Ingredients:

- 3 large apples, cored, diced
- 2 1/4 cups Arborio rice
- 4 1/2 cups milk
- 1 1/2 cups apple juice
- 3 tsp. ground cinnamon
- 1/2 cup brown sugar
- 3/4 cup dried cherries
- 3 tbsp. butter
- 1/2 tsp. salt or to taste
- Chopped almonds to serve

Method:

- Place a skillet with butter over medium heat. Add rice when the butter melts and sauté for 3-4 minutes. Transfer into the slow cooker.
- Add rest of the ingredients except cherries and stir.
- Cover and set on Low for 6 hours.
- Add cherries and mix well. Add more milk if you find it too dry.
- Serve topped with almonds.

Slow Cooked Carnitas

Ingredients

- 6 lbs. pork shoulder, lean only, trimmed of fat
- 2 onion, diced
- 2-4 diced chipotle peppers
- 1 ½ cup light beer or chicken broth
- 4 tbsp. adobo sauce
- 2 tsp. cumin
- 6-8 garlic cloves, minced
- 2-4 bay leaves
- 2 tsp. oregano
- 1 ½ tsp. salt
- 1 tsp. pepper

Method

1. Take the pork and season it with pepper and salt.
2. Place this in the slow cooker.
3. Take a bowl and mix the onion, garlic cloves, cumin, chipotle peppers, adobo sauce, and oregano, bay leaves and light beer or chicken broth.
4. Cook for 6-8 hours on Low until the pork is tender and it shreds easily.
5. In the meantime preheat the oven to 400 degrees F.
6. Lay the pork on a non-stick baking sheet in a single layer.
7. Roast it until the edges become toasted and crispy this should take about 4-5 minutes.
8. Serve hot.

Pizza in a Slow Cooker

Ingredients:

- 1 pound bulk Italian sausage, cooked
- 1 pound ground beef, cooked,
- 4 cups mozzarella cheese, shredded
- 1 jar (15 ounce) pizza sauce
- 3 cups fresh spinach
- 16 slices pepperoni
- ½ cup olives, sliced
- 1 cup mushrooms, sliced
- 1 green pepper, chopped
- 1 onion, chopped
- 2 cloves garlic, minced

Method:

1. Mix together sausage, ground beef, pizza sauce, and onions.
2. Add half of this mixture to the pot of the slow cooker.
3. Lay half of the spinach leaves over the mixture. Lay half of the pepperoni over the spinach. Sprinkle half of each of the following; olives, peppers, garlic, mushrooms, and mozzarella cheese.
4. Repeat step 2 with the remaining ingredients.
5. Close the pot and cook on low for 6-8 hours.
6. When done, cool it slightly and slice into 16 pieces.
7. Left over slices can be refrigerated and reheated.

Huevos Rancheros

Ingredients:

- 5 eggs
- 6 ounce Monterey Jack cheese, shredded
- 1/2 cup half and half
- 5 ounce taco sauce
- 2 scallions, sliced
- 1/2 a 4 ounce can chopped green chilies, drained
- 1 clove garlic, minced
- 1/4 tsp. black pepper powder
- 1/4 tsp. ancho chili powder
- Salt to taste
- 1 avocado, peeled, pitted, sliced
- 2 tbsp. fresh cilantro, chopped
- Juice of a lime
- Cooking spray
- 4 tortillas, warmed

Method:

1. Spray the inside of the slow cooker with cooking spray.
2. Add eggs to a bowl and whisk well along with half and half, 4 ounces of cheese, pepper powder, salt, and chili powder. Add garlic and green chilies. Fold gently and transfer into the slow cooker.
3. Cover and set on Low for 2 hours. Uncover and check after around 1 1/2 hours. If it is not set, then cook for another 30 minutes.
4. Pour taco sauce over the top of the set eggs and spread all over. Sprinkle the remaining cheese on top.
5. Cover and cook on Low for 15 minutes. Cut into 4-quarter pieces.
6. Place a piece over each of the tortillas. Sprinkle scallions and cilantro. Place avocado slices and finally sprinkle lemon juice and serve.

Pepperoncini Beef Sandwiches

Ingredients:

- 1 1/2 pounds beef chuck roast
- 2 cloves garlic, sliced
- 1/2 jar (8 ounce) pepperoncini
- 4 hoagie rolls, split lengthwise
- 8 slices provolone cheese
- Salt to taste
- Pepper powder to taste

Method:

1. Make small slits in the roast and insert the garlic slices in the slits.
2. Place the roast in a slow cooker. Add the pepperoncini along with the liquid over the meat.
3. Cover and set on Low for 6-8 hours.
4. Place meat in rolls along with the pepperoncini.
5. Sprinkle salt and pepper and top with cheese.
6. Microwave for a few seconds until the cheese melts and serve.

Chocolate Chip French toast

Ingredients:

- 6 cups French bread, cubed
- 1 cup milk
- 2 eggs
- 1 tsp. vanilla extract
- 1/3 cup semi-sweet chocolate chips
- 1/3 cup packed brown sugar
- 1 tsp. ground cinnamon

Method:

- Grease the inside of the slow cooker with oil. Place the bread at the bottom of the pot.
- Whisk together eggs, milk, sugar, vanilla and cinnamon in a bowl and pour over the bread. Stir, cover and chill overnight.
- Top with chocolate chips.
- Cover and set the pot on Low and cook for 4 hours.

Spinach and Mushroom Quiche

Ingredients:

- 3 1/2 cups frozen spinach
- 4 slices bacon, cooked crisp, crumbled
- 1 tbsp. olive oil
- 2 cups button mushrooms, chopped
- 1/2 cup red bell pepper, chopped
- 1 1/2 cups Swiss cheese or any other cheese, shredded
- 8 eggs
- 2 cups whole milk
- 2 tbsp. fresh chives, snipped
- Salt to taste
- Pepper to taste
- 1/2 cup packaged biscuit mix
- 1 disposable slow cooker liner
- Cooking spray

Method:

1. Line the slow cooker with the disposable liner.
2. Spray inside of the pot with cooking spray.
3. Squeeze the excess liquid from the spinach and place on paper towels.
4. Place a skillet with oil over medium heat. Add mushroom and bell pepper. Sauté until tender. Add spinach and cheese.
5. Meanwhile, in a bowl add eggs, milk, chives, salt and pepper. Whisk well.
6. Pour the egg mixture into the spinach mixture.
7. Add the biscuit mix and stir gently. Remove from heat and pour this mixture into the lined slow cooker.
8. Sprinkle bacon on top.
9. Cover and set the slow cooker on Low and cook for 4-5 hours or on High for 2-2 1/2 hours or a toothpick when inserted in the center should come out clean.
10. Cool for 15-20 minutes before serving. Slice into wedges and serve.

Slow Cooked Tacos

Ingredients

- 1 ounce lean sirloin roast, trimmed of fat
- 4 cloves garlic
- ½ tbsp. chili powder
- ½ onion, chopped
- 1 small bay leaf
- ½ tsp. black pepper
- ½ tbsp. smoked paprika
- ½ tsp. salt
- ½ cup beef broth

Method

1. Make a garlic paste either by pulsing the garlic in a blender, using a garlic press, or by mincing it and then pressing it into a paste using the back of knife, with a little coarse salt.
2. Create a rub by mixing together pepper, salt, paprika and chili powder into the garlic paste.
3. In the slow cooker add the onions and the beef broth. Place the tri-tip on it and cook on Low for 8 hours.
4. Remove the lid thirty minutes before the cooking time is finished and shred the meat. Cook it uncovered for thirty minutes.
5. Enjoy.

Chapter 8: Slow Cooker Soup and Stew Recipes

Mediterranean Stew

Ingredients:

- 1/2 butternut squash, peeled, deseeded, cubed
- 1 cup eggplants, cubed
- 1 cup zucchini, cubed
- 1/2 a 10 ounce package frozen okra, thawed
- 1/2 an 8 ounce can tomato sauce
- 1/2 cup onions, chopped
- 1 tomato, chopped
- 1 carrot, thinly sliced
- 1/2 cup low sodium vegetable broth
- 3 tbsp. raisins
- A large pinch cinnamon powder
- 1/4 tsp. turmeric powder
- Red chili flakes to taste
- 1/4 tsp. cumin powder
- A large pinch paprika

Method:

1. Add all the ingredients in the slow cooker.
2. Cover and set the cooker on Low for 8 hours or on High for 3-4 hours.
3. Serve in individual soup bowls.

Savory Cheese Soup

Ingredients:

- 7 ½ ounces broth (chicken or vegetable)
- 1 tbsp. red bell pepper, chopped
- 1 tbsp. onions, chopped
- 2 tbsp. celery, chopped
- 2 tbsp. carrots, chopped
- 1 tsp. butter
- A pinch black pepper powder
- 1 tbsp. all-purpose flour
- 1 tbsp. cold water
- 1 ½ ounces cream cheese, cubed
- 6 tbsp. cheddar cheese, shredded
- 3 tbsp. beer or extra broth
- Croutons to serve

Method:

1. Follow the manufacturer's instructions carefully and switch on the slow cooker.
2. Add all the ingredients except croutons to the slow cooker.
3. Stir, cover and cook on Low for 3-4 hours.
4. Serve hot soup in individual soup bowls with croutons.

Pork Chop Soup

Ingredients:

- 1 1/2 pounds pork chops
- 5 cups broth
- 1 1/2 (28 ounce each) cans diced tomatoes
- 1 1/2 cans (6 ounce each) tomato paste
- 1 large onion, chopped
- 1 1/2 cups V8 or vegetable juice
- 6 cloves garlic, minced
- 3 cups shell pasta, uncooked
- 1 1/2 tbsp. dried parsley
- 1 1/2 tbsp. dried basil
- Salt to taste
- Pepper powder to taste
- 1 1/2 cups water
- Shredded cheese to garnish

Method:

1. Add all the ingredients except pasta and mix well.
2. Cover and set on Low for about 7 hours or High for about 4 hours.
3. Add pasta. Mix well, cover and cook until the pasta is al dente.
4. If you find your soup too thick, add more broth or water.
5. Taste and adjust the seasonings if necessary.
6. Serve in individual soup bowls. Garnish with cheese and serve immediately.

Pumpkin Soup

Ingredients:

- 1 ½ medium sized butternut pumpkin, peeled, deseeded, chopped
- 4 potatoes, medium sized, chopped
- 2 onions, chopped
- 3 tsp. mild curry powder
- Salt to taste
- Crushed pepper to taste
- 5 cups vegetable stock
- 2 cups full cream
- ½ tsp. chili powder or to taste

Method:

1. Place in the slow cooker the pumpkin, onions, curry powder and stock.
2. Add salt and pepper.
3. Cover. Set on Low and cook for 5-6 hours or until the vegetables are tender.
4. When tender, switch off the heat. Keep aside to cool.
5. When cooled, transfer into the food processor and blend. Alternately you can use a stick blender. Blend until you get a smooth consistency
6. Add the cream and chili powder. Blend again.
7. Pour the soup into a saucepan and heat it to serve.

Potato and Corn Chowder

Ingredients:

- 12 ounces red potatoes, diced
- 8 ounces frozen corn
- 1 1/2 tbsp. all-purpose flour
- 4 cups chicken stock or any stock of your choice
- 1/2 tsp. onion powder
- 1/4 tsp. garlic powder
- 1/2 tsp. dried oregano
- 1/2 tsp. dried thyme
- Salt to taste
- Pepper powder to taste
- 2 tbsp. heavy cream
- 1 tbsp. unsalted butter

Method:

1. Follow the manufacturer's instructions carefully and switch on the slow cooker.
2. Whisk together about 1/2 a cup of stock and flour in a bowl and pour it into the slow cooker.
3. Add rest of the ingredients except cream and butter.
4. Stir, cover and cook on Low for 4 to 6 hours.
5. Add cream and butter. Mix well and serve immediately in individual soup bowls.

Onion Soup

Ingredients

- 32 ounces beef, vegetable, or chicken broth
- 1 tsp. brown sugar
- 2 sweet onions, sliced
- 11/2 garlic cloves, minced
- 1 tbsp. butter
- ½ tsp. pepper
- ½ tbsp. balsamic vinegar
- ½ tbsp. all-purpose flour
- ½ tbsp. Worcestershire sauce
- ½ tsp. salt
- 1 tbsp. fresh thyme

Method

1. Take a slow cooker and set it to High.
2. In it add the Worcestershire sauce, onions, salt, pepper, garlic, butter, brown sugar and vinegar.
3. Cook until the onions begin to brown and caramelize or cook for 60 minutes, stirring in between.
4. Add the flour and then cook for 5 minutes more.
5. Lastly add in the broth and thyme. Cook on Low for 6-8 hours.
6. Serve hot in individual soup bowls.

Fisherman Stew

Ingredients:

- 1 small white fish filled, deboned
- 6 scallops, cleaned
- 6 shrimp, peeled, deveined
- 6 clams, cleaned
- 6 mussels, cleaned
- 1 medium onion, chopped
- 2 cloves garlic, minced
- 1/2 a 28 ounce can crushed tomatoes with its juice
- 1/2 an 8 ounce can tomato sauce
- 1 green bell pepper, chopped
- 1 hot pepper, chopped
- 2 tbsp. fresh parsley, chopped
- 1/2 tsp. dried thyme
- 1 tsp. dried basil
- 1/2 tsp. dried oregano
- 1/4 tsp. cayenne pepper
- 1/4 tsp. paprika

Method:

1. Add all the ingredients except seafood to the slow cooker.
2. Cover and cook on Low for 4-5 hours or on High for 2-2 1/2 hours.
3. Add seafood and stir. Taste and adjust the seasonings if necessary.
4. Cover and cook on High for 30 minutes. Stir in between a couple of times while it is cooking.

Vegetable Minestrone Soup

Ingredients:

- 1 small onion, diced
- 2 medium carrots, peeled, sliced
- 2 cloves garlic, minced
- 1/2 a 28 ounce can diced tomatoes
- 1 can (15 ounce) cannellini beans, drained, rinsed
- 2 cups vegetable stock
- 2 cups water
- 1/2 cup frozen green peas
- 6 thin asparagus spears, stems removed, cut into thirds
- 4 ounces uncooked ditalini pasta
- 3 ounce fresh spinach
- 3 tbsp. freshly grated Romano cheese + extra for topping
- Salt to taste
- Pepper powder to taste

Method:

1. Add onion, carrots, garlic, tomatoes, beans, stock and water to the slow cooker.
2. Cover and cook on low for 5-6 hours.
3. During the last 15 - 50 minutes of cooking, add asparagus, spinach, peas, salt, pepper and pasta. Taste and adjust the seasoning.
4. Ladle into individual soup bowls. Garnish with cheese and serve immediately.

Lentil Soup

Ingredients:

- 2 brown onions, finely chopped
- 4 sticks celery, trimmed, chopped coarsely
- 2 carrots, peeled, coarsely chopped
- 2 cloves garlic, crushed
- 2 Swede, peeled, chopped coarsely
- 1 cup red lentils
- 4 cans tomatoes, diced
- 4 cups vegetable stock
- 6 tsp. cumin, powdered
- 2 baguette (French loaf), sliced thinly diagonally
- 7 oz. goat cheese
- ½ cup freshly chopped chives

Method:

1 In a slow cooker add onion, Swede, garlic, carrots, lentil, tomato, stock and cumin powder.
2 Cover. Set on High and cook for 3 hours or the vegetables are tender and the lentil is cooked well.
3 In a small bowl, add goat cheese and chives. Mix well.
4 Meanwhile, preheat a grill. Place the sliced baguette on the baking tray. Place the baking tray on the grill. Grill the loaf for 2 minutes or until the sides are golden.
5 Spread the cheese-chive mixture on the loaf slices. Serve hot with piping hot soup.

Baked Potato Soup

Ingredients:

- 2 pounds russet potatoes, peeled, chopped into small pieces
- 3 whole cloves garlic
- 4 cups chicken broth
- 1 medium onion, chopped
- 8 ounce low fat cream cheese
- 2 green onions, thinly sliced
- Salt to taste
- Pepper powder to taste

Method:

1. Follow the manufacturer's instructions carefully and switch on the slow cooker.
2. Add all the ingredients except cream cheese and green onions to the slow cooker.
3. Stir, cover and cook on Low for 7-8 hours or on High for 3-4 hours.
4. Retain about 1/4 of the soup and blend the rest of it with cream cheese.
5. Add green onions, reheat, mix well and serve.

Autumn Vegetable Beef Stew

Ingredients:

- 2 -3 pounds lean stew beef meat, cubed
- 4 cups beef broth
- 4 strips bacon, chopped
- 10 medium potatoes, diced
- 4 ribs celery, thinly sliced
- 4 medium carrots, thinly sliced
- 3 cups rutabaga, chopped
- 2 large onions, chopped
- 2 bay leaves
- Freshly ground pepper to taste
- Salt to taste
- 1 tsp. dried rosemary, crushed
- 4 tbsp. flour mixed with 1/2 cup water
- A handful parsley, chopped to garnish

Method:

1. Place a skillet over medium heat. Add onions, bacon, and beef and sauté for a few minutes until the beef is not pink any more.
2. Transfer into a slow cooker.
3. Add rest of the ingredients except the flour mixture.
4. Stir, cover and cook on Low for about 7 hours or on High for 3 1/2 to 4 hours.
5. Add flour mixture stir well.
6. Cook on High for 15-20 minutes. Stir, taste and adjust the seasonings if necessary.
7. Serve in individual soup bowls garnished with parsley.

Slow Cooker Taco Soup

Ingredients:

- ½ pound ground beef
- 1 medium onion, chopped
- ½ can (½ a 16 ounce can) chili beans, with liquid
- ½ can (½ a 15 ounce can) kidney beans with liquid
- ½ can (½ a 15 ounce) can whole kernel corn, with liquid
- ½ (½ a 8 ounce) can tomato sauce
- 1 cup water
- (14.5 ounce) can tomatoes, peeled, diced
- ½ can (2 ounce) green chili peppers, diced
- ½ package taco seasoning mix
- ½ cup Cheddar cheese, shredded
- Sour cream to garnish

Method:

1. Place a skillet over medium heat. Add ground beef.
2. Cook until browned. Drain and keep aside
3. Place the ground beef in a slow cooker.
4. Add onions, chili beans, kidney beans, corn, tomato sauce, water and tomatoes.
5. Also add the green chilli peppers and taco seasoning mix. Mix well.
6. Set the slow cooker on Low and cook for 8 hours.
   Serve topped with cheddar cheese and sour cream.

Turkish Lamb Stew:

Ingredients:

- ¾ pound lean leg of lamb, boneless, trimmed of fat, cut into 1 ½ inch pieces
- ¾ tsp. salt, divided
- Freshly ground pepper to taste
- 1 tbsp. extra virgin olive oil, divided
- 1 large onion, thinly sliced
- 2 cloves garlic, minced
- ¼ tsp. dried oregano
- 7 ounce canned tomatoes
- 1 medium potato, cut into thick slices
- ¼ pound green beans, trimmed
- 1 small eggplant, cut into thick slices
- 1 small zucchini, cut into thick slices
- 2 tbsp. fresh parsley, chopped

Method:

1. Sprinkle salt and pepper to the lamb.
2. Place a skillet over medium heat. Add half the oil. Add lamb and cook until brown on all the sides. Transfer it to the slow cooker.
3. Add the remaining oil to the skillet. Add onions and sauté until translucent. Add garlic and oregano and sauté for a minute. Add tomatoes and mix well. Crush it a little.
4. Use half of this mixture and coat the lamb with it.
5. Lay the potatoes. Sprinkle salt and pepper. Layer the vegetable slices over the potatoes. Over each layer, sprinkle salt and pepper.
6. Spread the remaining half of the tomato mixture over the last layer of vegetables. Place the bay leaves over it.
7. Cover and cook on LOW for 7 hours or on HIGH for 4 hours.
8. Remove the bay leaves and discard it.
9. Garnish with parsley and serve it.

Italian Soup:

Ingredients:

- 3 cups chicken stock or broth
- 2 cups water
- 1 egg
- 1 medium onion, chopped
- 2 cloves garlic, minced
- 1 stalk celery chopped
- 1 medium carrot, peeled, chopped
- 4 tbsp. sugar free marinara sauce
- ½ tsp. Italian seasoning
- Salt to taste
- Freshly ground pepper to taste
- ½ pound bulk Italian pork sausage
- ¼ pound ground beef chuck
- Cooking spray

Method:

1. Place a nonstick skillet over medium heat. Spray with cooking spray. Add onions, garlic celery, and carrots. Sauté for a couple of minutes and transfer to the slow cooker.
2. Add water, broth, sauce and seasoning.
3. Cover and cook on LOW for 7-8 hours.
4. Meanwhile, mix together sausage, beef, and egg. Mix well. Using your hands, shape the mixture into small balls and drop it to the boiling soup. Add salt and pepper.
5. Serve hot in bowls. Add more salt and pepper if necessary.

Lentil Cauliflower Stew:

Ingredients:

- 8 ounce dried lentils, picked, washed, soaked in a bowl of water
- ½ tbsp. olive oil
- 1 cup onions, chopped
- 2 cloves garlic, chopped
- ½ pound cauliflower, chopped into very small florets
- 1 leek, white and green parts, halved, chopped
- 1 large carrot, chopped
- 2 stalks celery, chopped
- 1 bay leaf
- ½ tsp. dried thyme
- Kosher salt to taste
- ½ tsp. cumin powder
- ½ tsp. cayenne pepper or to taste
- Black pepper powder to taste
- 4 cups low sodium vegetable broth
- 1 can (16 ounce) tomatoes, diced
- 1 cup kale or Swiss chard

Method:

1. Place a skillet over medium heat. Add onion and sauté until translucent. Add garlic and sauté for a couple of minutes. Transfer to the slow cooker.
2. Add rest of the ingredients.
3. Cover and cook on HIGH for 6 hours or LOW for 8 hours or until the lentils are done.
4. Serve garnished with cilantro.

Beef Stew:

Ingredients:

- 1 pound beef chuck, chopped into 1 ½ inch pieces
- ½ tsp. sweet paprika
- Salt to taste
- Freshly ground pepper to taste
- 3 tbsp. all-purpose flour+ extra to coat the beef
- 1 ½ tbsp. olive oil
- ½ pound small white potatoes, halved
- ¼ pound crimini mushrooms, halved
- 3 small carrots, chopped into 1 inch chunks
- 1 small onion, chopped
- 1 tbsp tomato paste
- ½ cup red wine
- 1 cup low sodium beef broth
- 2 sprigs fresh thyme
- ½ tsp. caraway seeds
- ¼ cup fresh parsley leaves, chopped
- 2 tbsp. sour cream

Method:

1. Season the beef with salt, pepper and paprika.
2. Place the flour in a plate. Dip the beef in flour. Coat well but remove the excess flour.
3. Place a nonstick skillet over medium heat. Add half the oil. Add beef and coon until browned on all the sides. Transfer the browned beef into the slow cooker.
4. Add potatoes, carrots, mushrooms, and onions. Mix well.
5. To the same skillet, add the remaining oil. Add the tomato paste and sauté for a minute. Add flour, wine and mix well. Add broth, thyme, caraway, salt, and pepper. Whisk constantly until thick gravy is formed.
6. Transfer the gravy into the slow cooker. Cover and cook on LOW for 7-8 hours or until done.
7. Add parsley and mix well.

Chapter 9: Slow Cooker Meat Recipes

Slow-Cooker Pepper Steak

Ingredients:

- 1 pound beef sirloin, cut into 2 inch strips
- 1 tsp. garlic powder or to taste
- 1 ½ tbsp. vegetable oil
- ½ cube beef bouillon
- 2 tbsp. hot water
- ½ tbsp. cornstarch
- ¼ cup chopped onion
- 1 large green bell peppers, roughly chopped
- ½ of a 14.5 ounce can stewed tomatoes, with liquid
- 1 ½ tbsp. soy sauce
- ½ tsp. sugar
- ½ tsp. salt

Method:

1. Sprinkle garlic powder over beef sirloin.
2. Over medium heat place a skillet. Add vegetable oil, heat. Add the beef sirloin.
3. Sauté until you brown it.
4. Transfer into a slow cooker.
5. Meanwhile in a bowl, add hot water and bouillon cube. When it is completely dissolved, add cornstarch. Mix well.
6. Pour this mix in the slow cooker.
7. Add onion, bell pepper, soy sauce, stewed tomatoes, salt and sugar.
8. Cover. Set on High and cook for 4 to 5 hours or set on Low and cook for 6 to 7 hours.

Lamb Paprikash

Ingredients:

- 1 lb. lamb, sliced into 1 inch pieces
- 7 oz. unsalted diced tomatoes
- 1/2 cup chopped onion
- 1/4 tsp minced garlic
- 1/2 tsp paprika
- 1/4 cup cold water
- 1/8 cup flour
- 1/4 cup fat free sour cream

Method:

1. Mix together the lamb, undrained tomatoes, garlic, paprika, and onion in the slow cooker.
2. Cover and cook for 8 hours on low, then increase the heat to high. Remove excess fat.
3. Combine the flour and cold water, then stir this into the mixture. Cover and cook for 20 minutes, or until thickened.
4. Take out about 1/4 cup of the liquid from the slow cooker and mix it with the sour cream in a bowl. Stir the mixture into the slow cooker and cook until heated.

Mexican Posole

Ingredients:

- 1 pound pork loin roast, boneless, cut into bite sized cubes
- 1 medium onion, sliced
- 1 can (15.5 ounce) white hominy, drained
- 1 can (14.5 ounce) enchilada sauce
- 3 cups water
- ½ tbsp. canola oil
- ¼ cup green chilies, sliced
- 2 cloves garlic, minced
- ¼ tsp. cayenne pepper or to taste
- 1 tsp. dried oregano
- Salt to taste
- 2 tbsp. fresh cilantro, chopped

Method:

1. Follow the manufacturer's instructions carefully and switch on the slow cooker.
2. Place a nonstick skillet over medium high heat. Add oil. When oil is heated, add pork loin roast and cook until brown. Transfer into the slow cooker.
3. Pour enchilada sauce over it. Spread hominy, onions, garlic, cayenne pepper and oregano over it.
4. Pour water, cover and cook on Low for 10-12 hours or on High for 5-6 hours.

Slow Cooker Shredded Beef Barbacoa

Ingredients

- 2 tsp. soy sauce, Magi, or fish sauce
- ¼ cup apple cider vinegar
- 2 whole dried New Mexico, seeds and stem removed
- 4 cups chicken broth
- 2 whole chili ancho or pasilla seeds and stem removed
- 2 tsp. vegetable oil
- Kosher salt
- 2 small onion
- 8 garlic cloves
- 4 canned chipotle chilies and 2 tbsp. adobo sauce
- 2 tsp. cumin
- 5 lbs. lean beef round or brisket
- 1 tsp. allspice
- 2 bay leaf
- 2 tsp. oregano
- 2 whole chili negro, seeds and stem removed

Method

1. Take a medium sized pot and heat it on medium heat. Toast the dried chilies until they turn brown or for about 3 minutes. Add two cups chicken broth and allow it to boil. Once it boils, lower the heat and allow it to cook for 15 minutes until they become tender.
2. In the meantime heat vegetable oil in a pan over medium heat. Add the onion and cook until they soften and begin to brown, this will take about 10 minutes.
3. Add in the oregano, allspice, cumin, garlic, adobo sauce and chipotles. Cook for another 2 minutes. Lastly add the apple cider vinegar and soya sauce. Turn the heat off and scrape everything from the bottom of the pan.
4. In a blender add the cooked dried chilies and the broth. Also add in the onion mixture. Blend it well.
5. Take a slow cooker and add the beef seasoned with salt and pepper. Add in the Barbacoa salsa from the blender. Cook in the slow cooker for 6-8 hours.
6. In the last 30 minutes remove the lid from the slow cooker and shred the beef so that the beef can absorb the sauce.
7. Serve hot.

Leg of Lamb:

Ingredients:

- 1 ¾ pounds leg of lamb (bone out)
- 2 tbsp. olive oil
- 4 tbsp. lemon juice
- 3 cloves garlic, crushed
- ½ tsp. dried oregano
- ½ tsp. nutmeg
- 1 tsp. dried mint
- ½ tsp. sugar
- 2 tbsp. white vinegar

Method:

1. Mix together oil, lemon juice, oregano, garlic and nutmeg in the slow cooker.
2. Add the lamb to the mixture. Let it dip on all the sides.
3. Cover and cook on LOW for 7-8 hours or until the bones are just about to come out.
4. Remove the lamb from the cooker. Using forks, remove the meat from the bones.
5. In a microwavable bowl, mix together mint, sugar, and vinegar. Microwave on high for 30 seconds.
6. Pour this mixture over the lamb and serve.

Spaghetti squash and Meatballs

Ingredients:

- 2 pounds ground Italian sausage
- 2 medium spaghetti squash, halved, deseeded
- 2 cans (14 ounce each) tomato sauce
- 1 tsp. dried oregano
- 1 tsp. dried basil
- 1 tsp. thyme
- 8 cloves garlic, whole
- 4 tbsp. hot pepper relish (optional)
- 4 tbsp. olive oil
- 2 tbsp. fresh parsley, chopped

Method:

1. Follow the manufacturer's instructions carefully and switch on the slow cooker.
2. Add olive oil, tomato sauce, garlic, hot pepper relish, oregano, basil, and thyme to the cooker. Mix well.
3. Place the spaghetti squash halves in the cooker with its cut side down.
4. Meanwhile, make small meatballs with the ground meat and place it all around the squash.
5. Cover and set the cooker on Low for 4-5 hours or on High for 3 hours.
6. When done, remove the squash from the pot. When cool enough to handle, pull out the flesh from the squash using a large fork.
7. Place the squash flesh on a serving platter. Top with the meatballs. Pour the sauce all over. Garnish with parsley and serve hot.

Moroccan Lamb

Ingredients:

- 1 whole lamb shank, trimmed of fat
- 1 medium onion, chopped
- 1 small red bell pepper, chopped
- 1/2 a 14 ounce can diced tomatoes
- 1/4 cup whole olives, drained
- 1/2 cup canned garbanzo beans, rinsed, drained
- 1/2 lemon, chopped into pieces
- 2 cloves garlic, minced
- 1/2 tsp. sugar
- 1/2 tsp. ground cumin
- 1/2 tsp. ground coriander
- Salt and pepper powder to taste
- 1 cup water
- 2 tsp. olive oil
- 1 stick cinnamon (about an inch)
- 2 tbsp. golden raisins

Method:

1. Mix together in a bowl, lemon, sugar and salt and set aside.
2. Season the lamb shank with salt and pepper.
3. Place a skillet with oil over medium heat. Add lamb shank and brown on all the sides. Remove from the pan and set aside.
4. To the same pan, add onions, bell pepper and garlic. Sauté for a couple of minutes and transfer into the slow cooker.
5. Add rest of the ingredients except raisins and mix well. Add lamb and coat it with the mixture in the pot.
6. Cover and cook on Low for 8-9 hours or on High for 4-5 hours.
7. Half way through cooking, add raisins and the lemon mixture to it. Mix well and cover again.
8. When done, discard cinnamon and the lemon pieces and serve.

Slow Cooked Pulled BBQ Pork

Ingredients

- 1/2 (14 ounce) can beef broth
- 1/2 (18 ounce) bottle barbeque sauce
- 1 1/2 pounds boneless pork ribs

Method:

1. Place the boneless pork ribs in the bottom of a slow cooker.
2. Gently pour the beef broth over the pork ribs.
3. Cover and cook on the High setting for about 4 hours or until the meat is extremely tender and can be shredded easily.
4. Remove the pork ribs from the slow cooker and place in a flat dish.
5. Once cool enough to handle, use two forks to gently shred the pork ribs.
6. Crank up your oven to 350 degrees Fahrenheit (about 175 degrees Celsius) and let it preheat for about 20 minutes.
7. Place the shredded pork ribs in a cast iron skillet or in a Dutch oven and add the barbeque sauce to it.
8. Mix well and pop the baking dish into the preheated oven and bake for about 30 to 35 minutes or until the pork is thoroughly heated.
9. Serve hot in a gluten free bun.
   Enjoy!

Szechuan Pork

Ingredients:

- 3 pounds lean pork chops, boneless, trimmed of fat
- 2 cans (8 ounce each) sliced water chestnuts, drained
- 2 cans (8 ounce each) sliced bamboo shoots, drained
- 12 green onions, sliced
- 3 tbsp. garlic, minced
- 4 tbsp. ginger, minced
- ½ cup soy sauce
- ½ cup Szechuan hot bean paste or sauce
- ½ cup Worcestershire sauce
- 4 tbsp. sesame oil
- 4 tbsp. rice wine or dry sherry
- 3 tbsp. sesame oil
- 3 tbsp. sugar
- 2 tsp. hot sauce (optional)

Method:

1. Follow the manufacturer's instructions carefully and switch on the slow cooker.
2. Place a nonstick skillet over medium high heat. Add pork chops and cook until brown. Transfer into the slow cooker.
3. Place bamboo shoots over the chops, followed by water chestnuts and green onions.
4. Mix together rest of the ingredients in a bowl and pour it over the vegetables in the slow cooker.
5. Cover and cook on Low for 6-7 hours or on High for 3-4 hours.
6. Serve hot with steamed rice.

Braised Lamb Shanks

Ingredients:

- 6 lamb shanks, trimmed of fat
- 1 large onion, chopped
- 3 carrots, peeled, chopped
- 3 stalks celery, chopped
- 1 ½ cups ripe tomatoes, peeled, deseeded, chopped
- 5 cloves garlic, crushed
- 3 cups chicken stock
- 3 tbsp. tomato paste
- 2 tsp. fresh thyme
- 2 bay leaves
- 3 tbsp. olive oil
- 1 ½ cups red wine
- Salt to taste
- Pepper powder to taste

Method:

1. Follow the manufacturer's instructions carefully and switch on the slow cooker.
2. Sprinkle salt and pepper over the lamb shanks.
3. Place a nonstick skillet over medium high heat. Add oil. When oil is heated, add lamb shanks and cook until brown. Transfer into the slow cooker.
4. Add wine to the skillet and place over medium heat. Scrape any brown bits from the bottom of the skillet. Simmer for a couple of minutes and transfer into the slow cooker.
5. Add rest of the ingredients.
6. Stir, cover and cook on High for 6-7 hours. When done, transfer on to a serving dish.
7. Discard the bay leaf. Blend the remaining ingredients of the slow cooker until smooth.
   Pour over the shanks and serve.

Hungarian Beef Goulash:

Ingredients:

- 1 pound beef stew meat, trimmed of fat, cubed
- 1 medium onion, chopped
- 1 small red bell pepper, chopped
- 1 tsp. caraway seeds
- 1/4 tsp. salt or to taste
- Freshly ground pepper powder to taste
- 1/2 a 14 ounce can low sodium beef broth
- 1/2 a 14 ounce can diced tomatoes
- 1 tsp. Worcestershire sauce
- 2 cloves garlic, minced
- 1 bay leaf
- 1/2 tbsp. cornstarch
- 1 tbsp. water
- 1 tbsp. fresh parsley, chopped

Method:

1. Crush the caraway seeds. Mix together in a bowl, caraway seeds, paprika, salt, and pepper.
2. Sprinkle spice mixture all over beef.
3. Place the beef in a slow cooker. Place onions and bell pepper over the beef.
4. Pour broth and Worcestershire sauce to a saucepan. Add garlic and tomatoes. Place the pan over medium heat and simmer for 5 minutes. Pour this mixture over the beef in the cooker. Add bay leaf.
5. Cover and cook on Low for 7 - 8 hours or on High for 4 - 5 hours.
6. Remove and discard the bay leaves.
7. Mix cornstarch and water in a bowl. Pour in the cooker. Stir well and cook on high for about 10 minutes until the sauce thickens.
8. Garnish with parsley and serve.

Cauliflower Beef

Ingredients:

- 3/4 pound flank steak, thinly sliced, chopped into 2 inch pieces
- 1/2 cup vegetable broth
- 4 cups cauliflower florets
- 1/3 cup low sodium soy sauce
- 1/4 cup brown sugar
- 1/2 tbsp. garlic, minced
- 1/2 tbsp. sesame oil
- 1/4 tsp. red chili flakes or to taste
- 1 tbsp. corn starch mixed with 2 tbsp. cold water
- Salt to taste
- Cooking spray

Method:

1. Spray inside of the slow cooker with cooking spray.
2. Add all the ingredients except cornstarch mixture and cauliflower to the slow cooker.
3. Cover and cook on Low for 4 - 5 hours or on High for 2-3 hours.
4. Add cauliflower and cornstarch mixture. Mix well.
5. Cover and cook on Low for 30 -40 minutes.
6. Mix well and serve hot.

Slow Cooker Falling Off the Bone Short Ribs

Ingredients:

- 1 ¼ pounds beef short ribs
- 1 tsp. dried rosemary
- 2 tsp. dried thyme
- Freshly ground black pepper
- Salt to taste
- 1 tbsp. ground porcini mushroom or dried mushroom powder
- 1 tbsp. olive oil
- 1 medium onion, chopped
- 1 small fennel bulb, trimmed, cored, chopped
- 1 small carrot, chopped
- 1 celery stalk, chopped
- 2 cloves garlic, chopped
- ½ cup red wine
- ¾ cup chicken stock
- 1 tbsp. all-purpose flour
- 2 tsp. tomato paste
- Bouquet garni made of 2 sprigs thyme, 1 small bay leaf, 2 sprigs parsley, 1 small rosemary sprig, fastened with a string

Method:

1. Place a pot filled with water and short ribs over medium heat. Bring to the boil. Continue boiling for 4-5 minutes.
2. Remove from heat and discard all the water. Place on paper towels for a while and dry with paper towels.
3. Sprinkle salt and pepper over the ribs.
4. Mix together in a bowl, dried thyme, rosemary, flour and ground mushroom. Dredge the ribs in this mixture and set aside.
5. Place a skillet over medium heat. Add oil. When the oil is heated, place the ribs and cook until brown on all sides. Remove the ribs with a slotted spoon and place in the slow cooker.
6. Discard most of the fat that is remaining in the skillet.
7. Add celery, carrot, onion and fennel for 4-5 minutes. Add garlic and sauté for a couple of minutes. Sprinkle salt and pepper and transfer into the slow cooker.

8. Place the skillet back on heat. Add wine and tomato taste and scrape the bottom of the pan to remove any browned bits that are stuck to the bottom.
9. Pour into the slow cooker. Place the bouquet garni in it. Pour stock into it. Stir.
10. Close the lid of the slow cooker. Select 'Low' option and set the timer for 8-10 hours or until done.
11. Remove ribs with a slotted spoon and place on a plate. Cover loosely with a foil.
12. Strain the liquid in the cooker into a saucepan. Discard the solids that are left behind in the strainer. Also discard the fat that is floating on the top of the liquid.
13. Place the saucepan over medium heat and simmer until slightly thick. Pour over the ribs and serve with potatoes or rice.

Mexican Chuck Roast

Ingredients

- 1 (2 pound) chuck roast
- 1/2 tsp. ground black pepper
- 1/2 tsp. salt
- 1 tbsp. olive oil
- 10 tbsp. diced green chili pepper
- 1/2 large onion, chopped
- 1/2 tsp. chili powder
- 1/2 (5 ounce) bottle hot pepper sauce
- 1/2 tsp. ground cayenne pepper
- 1/2 tsp. garlic powder

Method:

1. Trim all the extra fat from the chuck roast and sprinkle salt and pepper over it. Use your fingers to lightly rub the salt and pepper into the roast.
2. Pour the olive oil into a large skillet and heat over a medium high flame until it is lightly smoking.
3. Add the chuck roast to the skillet and cook until well browned on all sides.
4. Transfer the browned beef to the bottom of a slow cooker and top it with the chopped onion.
5. Add in the green chili pepper, cayenne pepper, garlic powder, chili powder and hot pepper sauce over the chuck roast.
6. Pour in enough water so that about 1/3rd of the roast is covered.
7. Cover the Slow Cooker, and cook on the High setting for about 6 hours, checking every hour if there is enough cooking liquid in the slow cooker. If all the liquid is gone, add in a little at a time to keep the chuck roast moist and juicy.
8. At the end of 6 hours, lower the heat setting and continue cooking for another 3 to 4 hours or until the roast is tender enough to fall apart.
9. Transfer the meat to a bowl and shred using two forks.
10. Pour the cooking liquid into a skillet and heat until bubbling. Reduce the heat to a low flame and continue simmering the liquid until it thickens and is thick enough to coat the back of the spoon.
11. Add the shredded meat to the sauce and mix well.
12. Spoon into some gluten free tacos or gluten free tortillas and serve hot.
13. Enjoy!

Super Easy Country Style Ribs

Ingredients:

- 1 pound country style pork ribs, boneless
- 3/4 cup ketchup
- 1/4 cup vinegar
- 1/4 cup brown sugar
- 1/4 tsp. liquid smoke
- 1 tsp. seasoned salt

Method:

- Add all the ingredients to the slow cooker.
- Cover and cook on Low for 10-11 hours or on High for 5-6 hours.
- Remove the ribs with a slotted spoon and place on a serving platter. Pour the juices into a small pan. Set aside for 10 minutes. Discard the fat that will float on top.
- Place the pan over medium heat and bring to the boil.
- Boil until the gravy is thickened.
- Slice the roast. Pour sauce over the roast and serve.

Salisbury steak

Ingredients:

- 1 pound lean ground beef
- ½ envelope (½ ounce) dry onion soup mix
- ¼ cup Italian seasoned bread crumbs
- 2 tbsp. milk
- 2 tbsp. all-purpose flour
- 1 tbsp. vegetable oil
- 1 (10.75 ounce) can condensed cream of chicken soup
- ½ packet (½ ounce) dry au jus mix
- 6 tbsp. water

Method:

1. Mix together in a bowl, the ground beef, onion soup mix, breadcrumbs and milk. Mix well with your hands. Make patties.
2. Place a skillet over medium high heat. Add oil. Heat.
3. Coat the patties with flour. Place it in the skillet. Brown the patties.
4. Stack the patties in the slow cooker.
5. Meanwhile mix together in a bowl, the cream of chicken soup, au jus mix and water. Pour this mixture over the stacked patties.

Chapter 10: Slow Cooker Poultry Recipes

Sesame – Ginger Chicken

Ingredients:

- ½ tbsp. sesame oil
- 4 bone in chicken thighs, skinned
- 1 tbsp. vegetable oil
- 2 tbsp. low tamari sauce
- 1 tbsp. coconut sugar
- 1 tbsp. fresh orange juice
- 2 ½ tsp. hoisin sauce
- 1 tbsp. ginger, minced
- 2 cloves garlic
- ½ tbsp. arrowroot
- ½ tbsp. water
- 1 tsp. sesame seeds toasted
- 1 tbsp. green onion, sliced
- Cooking spray

Method:

1. Place a nonstick skillet over medium heat. Add oil and heat. Add chicken and cook on both sides until golden brown.
2. Spray the slow cooker with oil. Place the browned chicken in the cooker.
3. Mix together tamari sauce, coconut sugar, orange juice, hoisin sauce, ginger, and garlic. Pour this over the chicken. Cover.
4. Set the cooker on Low for 2 ½ to 3 hours. Transfer the chicken on to a platter and keep warm.
5. Strain the remaining liquid in the cooker and place in a pan (it should measure at least ½ to ¾ cup otherwise add water). Discard the solids.
6. Heat the saucepan over medium heat and bring to a boil. Mix together arrowroot and water in a small bowl. Add this to the saucepan. Stir constantly until thickened. Bring back to a boil.
7. Pour sauce over the chicken.

8. Sprinkle sesame seeds and green onions.

Creamy Chicken and Mushroom Potpie

Ingredients:

- 16 ounces cremini mushrooms, stems trimmed, halved if the mushrooms are large
- 8 carrots, peeled, cut into 1 inch pieces
- 3 pounds chicken thighs, skinless, boneless
- 1 large onion, chopped
- 2/3 cup all-purpose flour
- 2 sheets puff pastry, thawed
- 2 cups frozen green beans
- 2 cups frozen green peas
- 2 bay leaves
- 1 tsp. dried thyme
- 1 cup water
- Salt to taste
- Pepper powder to taste
- ¼ cup cream

Method:

1. Follow the manufacturer's instructions carefully and switch on the slow cooker.
2. Add onions, mushrooms, carrots, onion, all-purpose flour, thyme, bay leaves and water to the slow cooker. Stir the contents well.
3. Lay the chicken thighs over the vegetable mixture. Sprinkle salt and pepper over the chicken as well as over the vegetables.
4. Cover and cook on Low for 7 – 8 hours or on High for 4 – 5 hours.
5. When done, switch off the slow cooker and keep it covered.
6. Cut the pastry sheets with a 4-½ inch cutter into 4 circles. Place the circles on a baking sheet and bake in a preheated oven at 425 degree F for about 8 – 10 minutes.
7. Just before serving, add peas, green beans, cream and salt to the slow cooker.
8. Cover and heat the contents thoroughly.
9. Divide and serve chicken along with vegetables in individual serving bowls. Place a baked pastry round over each bowl and serve.

11. Close the lid of the slow cooker. Select 'Low' option and set the timer for 3-4 hours or until done.
12. Carefully remove the turkey fillet from the slow cooker and place on a plate. Cover with foil. Set aside for some time.
13. Meanwhile, strain the liquid that is remaining in the cooking pot into a pan. Retain the cooked vegetables. Mix together in a bowl flour and 2-3 tbsp. water and add into the pan.
14. Place the pan on medium heat. Stir constantly until it thickens.
15. Lower heat and simmer for a few minutes.
16. Slice the turkey breast and place on a serving platter. Pour the cooked sauce on the turkey slices and top with the cooked vegetables.
17. Sprinkle thyme and some more pepper on it and serve.

Chicken Pad Thai:

Ingredients:

- 1 ½ pounds chicken, skinless, thighs or breasts
- 1 medium zucchini
- 1 medium carrot, shredded
- ½ cup bean sprouts
- 1 cup green onions, chopped
- ¾ cup coconut milk
- ½ cup chicken stock
- 1 ½ tbsp. sunflower butter
- ½ tbsp. gluten free tamari
- 1 tsp. fish sauce
- ½ tbsp. ginger, minced
- 2 cloves garlic, minced
- ½ tsp. cayenne pepper
- ½ tsp. red pepper flakes
- Salt to taste
- Pepper powder to taste
- 2 tbsp. cilantro, chopped

Method:

1. Mix together salt, pepper, cayenne pepper, and ginger. Rub this mixture on to the chicken.
2. Add chicken stock and coconut milk to the slow cooker. Mix well until they are well blended.
3. Add sunflower butter, tamari, fish sauce, garlic, green onions, some more pepper, and cayenne pepper to taste. Mix well until the whole mixture is well blended and the sunflower butter is dissolved.
4. Transfer the chicken to the cooker.
5. Cover and cook on LOW for 3 ½ hours on LOW.
6. Meanwhile make zucchini noodles with a spiral slicer. Mix together the noodles, carrots and bean sprouts.
7. Lay the noodle mixture over the chicken and cook for 30-40 minutes more until the noodles are just steamed.

8. When done, remove the noodle mixture and keep aside on a plate.
9. Place the chicken pieces over the noodles. Remove some of the liquid from the cooker and pour over the chicken.
10. Garnish with some green onions and cilantro.

Oriental Ginger Chicken

Ingredients:

- 3 boneless and skinless chicken breasts, cubed
- 1/2 cup diced carrots
- 1/4 cup low sodium soy sauce
- 1/8 cup chopped onion
- 1/8 cup rice vinegar
- 1/2 Tbsp. ground ginger
- 1/8 cup sesame seeds
- 1/2 tsp sesame oil
- 1/2 cup cauliflower
- 1/2 cup broccoli

Method:

1. Brown the chicken breasts in a greased skillet over medium high flame, then transfer into the slow cooker.
2. Add the rest of the ingredients, except the cauliflower and broccoli, into the slow cooker. Cover and cook for 4 hours on low.
3. Add the cauliflower and broccoli and mix well. Cook for an additional hour, then serve.

Turkey Stew with Roasted Hatch chilies

Ingredients:

- 2 pounds free-range ground turkey or ground beef if you prefer beef
- 1 tbsp. extra-virgin olive oil
- 2 cloves garlic, chopped
- 1 medium red onion, chopped
- 1 cup roasted Hatch chilies, chopped
- 1 medium, peeled, cubed
- 1 ear of fresh sweet corn, cut off the cob
- ½ a 14-oz can fire roasted diced tomatoes
- 2 cups broth, or more if needed
- ½ tsp. cumin
- ½ tsp. ground coriander
- Sea salt to taste
- Ground pepper, to taste
- Juice of a lime
- Avocado, sliced to serve
- Sour cream to serve (optional)
- Fresh cilantro to serve

Method:

1. To roast the chilies: Take some Mexican Hatch chilies and roast in the oven at 450 degrees for about 7 minutes. Alternately you can grill the chilies or sauté in a pan on high heat for about 10 minutes.
2. Follow the manufacturer's instructions carefully and switch on the slow cooker.
3. Place a skillet over medium heat. Add the ground turkey and cook until browned. Transfer the turkey into the slow cooker.
4. Add rest of the ingredients except lime, avocado, sour cream, and cilantro.
5. Stir, cover and cook on Low for 7-8 hours or on High for 3-4 hours.
6. When done add lime juice and sprinkle cilantro.
7. Serve with sour cream and avocado.

Asian Braised Turkey with vegetables:

Ingredients:

- 1 package (3 ½ ounce) shiitake mushrooms, remove stems, slice
- ½ cup thinly sliced red bell pepper
- 3 baby bok choy, quartered lengthwise
- 3 bamboo shoots, sliced
- ½ a 15 ounce can precut baby corn, drained
- 1 tbsp. Hoisin sauce
- 1 tbsp. oyster sauce
- ½ tbsp. low sodium soy sauce
- 1 tsp. fresh grated ginger
- 1 tsp. dark sesame oil
- 2 cloves garlic, minced
- ½ tbsp. canola oil
- 2 pounds bone-in turkey thighs, skinned
- ½ tsp. 5 spice powder
- ¼ tsp. freshly ground pepper
- 1 cup thinly sliced Napa cabbage
- ¼ cup chopped green onions

Method:

1. Place a nonstick pan over medium heat. Add canola oil and heat. Meanwhile season the turkey thighs with 5-spice powder and pepper. Add the turkey to the pan. If the quantity is too much for your pan, then do it in batches. Brown the turkey on both the sides until browned.
2. Add mushrooms, bell pepper, bok choy, baby corn, and bamboo shoots to the slow cooker.
3. Add the browned turkey to the cooker.
4. Mix together in a bowl, all the sauces, ginger, garlic, and sesame oil. Pour this over the vegetables in the cooker.
5. Cover and cook on low for 5 hours or until the turkey is done.

6. Separate the turkey from the bones and discard the bones. Cut the turkey into bite size pieces.
7. To the cooker, add cabbage and mix well.
8. Pour into individual bowls. Place the chopped turkey over the vegetables and sprinkle with green onions.

Sweet n Sour Chicken

Ingredients:

- 6 chicken breasts, skinless, boneless, thawed if frozen
- 22 ounces canned pineapple chunks
- 3 green bell peppers, chopped into 1/2 inch squares
- 1 large onion, chopped into 1/2 inch squares
- 15 ounces sweet and sour sauce

Method:

1. Add chicken to the slow cooker. Pour only the juice from the pineapple can into the pot.
2. Cover and cook on Low for 5-6 hours or on High for 2 1/2 -3 hours or until done.
3. Drain the liquid that is remaining in the pot.
4. Mix together rest of the ingredients in a bowl and pour on top of the chicken. Stir well.
5. Cover and cook on High for 30 minutes.

Slow cooked Herby Turkey Breast

Ingredients:

- 2 small onions, quartered
- 2 1/2 - 3 pounds bone in whole turkey breast with skin
- 1 bay leaf
- 1/2 cup low sodium chicken broth
- 1/2 tbsp. dried sage
- 1/2 tbsp. dried rosemary
- 1/2 tbsp. dried thyme
- 1 tsp. onion powder
- 1 tsp. garlic powder
- 1/2 tbsp. corn starch mixed with about 2 tbsp. water
- Freshly ground black pepper to taste
- Salt to taste

Method:

1. Place the onion and bay leaf in the slow cooker. Place the turkey breast with the breast side down over the onions.
2. Sprinkle rest of the ingredients except cornstarch.
3. Cover and cook on Low for 7-8 hours or until done.
4. Transfer the turkey on to your cutting board.
5. Strain the liquid and set aside for about 5-7 minutes. Discard the spices and discard the floating fat and add the liquid to a saucepan.
6. Place the saucepan over medium heat. Cook until slightly thick.
7. Add the cornstarch mixture and stir constantly until thickened. Pour over the cooked turkey and serve.

Indian Butter Chicken:

Ingredients:

- 1 pound chicken breasts, cubed
- ½ tbsp. vegetable oil
- 1 shallot, finely chopped
- 1 onion, chopped
- 1 tbsp. butter
- 1 tsp. lemon juice
- 2 cloves garlic, minced
- ½ inch piece ginger, minced
- 1 tsp. garam masala (Indian spice blend)
- ½ tsp. chili powder
- ½ tsp. ground cumin
- 1 bay leaf
- 2 tbsp. plain nonfat yogurt
- 2 tbsp. half and half
- 6 tbsp. skim milk
- ½ cup tomato sauce
- 1 tsp. cayenne pepper or to taste
- Salt to taste
- 1/8 tsp. pepper powder
- Cilantro leaves for garnishing

Method:

1. Place a skillet over medium heat. Add oil. When oil is heated, add onions and shallot and sauté until translucent.
2. Add ginger and garlic and sauté for a couple of minutes. Add garam masala, cumin, cayenne, chili powder, and bay leaf. Sauté for a few seconds. Add tomato sauce, milk, half and half and yogurt. Lower heat and simmer for 5-6 minutes. Stir on and off.
3. Remove from heat. Add salt and pepper. Cool slightly and blend in a blender or with a stick blender until smooth

4. Add the chicken pieces to the slow cooker. Pour the blended mixture to the cooker. Mix well.
5. Cover and cook for 4 hours on low or until done.
6. Garnish with cilantro leaves and serve hot with steamed rice.

Chapter 11: Slow Cooker Seafood Recipes

Shrimp Creole

Ingredients:

- 3 pounds shrimp, peeled, deveined
- 3 large onions, chopped
- 3 cups celery, diced
- 1 large green bell pepper, chopped
- 1 large red bell pepper, chopped
- 2 cans (28 ounces each) whole tomatoes, crushed
- 2 cans (8 ounces each) tomato sauce
- 1 tsp. Creole seasoning
- 2 cloves garlic, minced
- Salt and pepper to taste
- 1 tsp. Tabasco sauce

Method:

1. Add all the ingredients except shrimp to the slow cooker and stir.
2. Cover and cook on High for 3-4 hours or on Low for 6-7 hours.
3. Add shrimp during the last 40 minutes of cooking.
4. Serve hot over rice.

Shrimp and Artichoke Barley Risotto

Ingredients:

- 1 1/2 cups onions, chopped
- 1 tbsp. olive oil
- 1 1/2 packages (9 ounce each) frozen artichoke hearts, thawed, quartered
- 4 1/2 cups boiling water
- 2 tbsp. Better than Bouillon Lobster Base
- 5 cloves garlic, mined
- 1 1/2 cups pearl barley
- 1 1/2 pounds shrimp, peeled deveined
- 6 ounce baby spinach
- 3 ounce parmesan cheese, grated
- 3 tsp. lemon zest, grated
- Freshly ground black pepper to taste
- Salt to taste

Method:

1. Add lobster base to boiling water. Whisk well and keep it aside.
2. Place a nonstick skillet over low heat. Add oil and onions and sauté until it gets translucent.
3. Then add garlic and sauté until fragrant. Transfer into the slow cooker.
4. Add lobster base solution and rest of the ingredients except spinach, lemon zest, cheese, and shrimp.
5. Cover and cook on Low for 6 hours or on High for 3 hours.
6. During the last 15 minutes of cooking, add shrimp and cheese and stir.
7. Cover and cook on High for 15 minutes.
8. Add lemon zest and baby spinach. Mix well. Taste and adjust the seasoning and serve.

Slow cooked Tilapia

Ingredients:

- 8 tilapia fillets
- 2 tsp. garlic, minced
- 4 tbsp. garlic butter, chopped into 8 small cubes
- 2 tsp. parsley, minced
- Salt to taste
- Pepper powder to taste

Method:

1. Lay the fillets in the slow cooker. Sprinkle salt and pepper over it.
2. Place a cube of butter on each of the fillets. Sprinkle the minced garlic and parsley over the fish.
3. Wrap an aluminum foil all around the fish. Seal it well.
4. Cover and cook on Low for 4 hours or on High for 2 hours

Beer Potato Fish

Ingredients:

- 1 1/2 pounds fish fillet
- 1 1/2 cups beer
- 6 medium potatoes, cubed
- 1 large red pepper, sliced
- 1 1/2 tbsp. oyster sauce
- 1 1/2 tbsp. oil
- 1 1/2 tbsp. rock candy
- Salt to taste

Method:

1. Add all the ingredients to slow cooker.
2. Cover and cook on High for 45 minutes.

Simple Poached Salmon

Ingredients:

- 6 salmon fillets (6 ounces each)
- 3/4 cup water
- 2 slices yellow onion
- 3/4 cup dry white wine
- Salt and pepper to taste
- 2 sprigs dill

Method:

1. Add water and wine to the slow cooker. Cover and cook on High for 20-30 minutes.
2. Add rest of the ingredients.
3. Cover and cook on High for 20 minutes.
4. Serve either hot or cold.

Tuna Casserole

Ingredients:

- 4 cans (7 ounces each) tuna, drained
- 4 cans cream of celery soup
- 2 packages frozen peas, thawed
- 2/3 cup chicken broth
- 1/3 cup buttered bread crumbs or crumbled potato chips
- 1 1/3 cups milk
- 20 ounces egg noodles, cook according to the instructions on the package
- 4 tbsp. dried parsley flakes
- Salt to taste
- Pepper powder to taste
- Cooking spray

Method:

1. Spray the inside of the slow cooker with cooking spray.
2. Add soup, broth, milk, parsley flakes, peas and tuna to the slow cooker. Stir well.
3. Add noodles and fold gently.
4. Sprinkle breadcrumbs.
5. Cover and cook on Low for 5-6 or on High for 3 hours.

Citrus Fish

Ingredients:

- 2 pounds fish fillets
- 1 large onion, chopped
- 3 tsp. orange zest, grated
- 3 tsp. lemon zest, grated
- 1/3 cup fresh parsley, chopped + extra for garnishing
- Salt and pepper to taste
- 2 tbsp. vegetable oil
- 1 orange, thinly sliced
- 1 lemon, thinly sliced
- Cooking spray

Method:

1. Spray the inside of the slow cooker with cooking spray. Sprinkle salt and pepper over the fish fillets and place in the slow cooker.
2. Sprinkle onions, parsley, orange zest, lemon zest and oil over it.
3. Cover and cook on Low for 1 1/2 hours.
4. Sprinkle fresh parsley. Place orange and lemon slices on top and serve.

Chapter 12: Slow Cooker Vegetarian Recipes

Broccoli and Rice Casserole:

Ingredients:

- 3/4 cup brown rice, uncooked
- 1 1/4 cup water
- 1/4 cup mushrooms, finely chopped
- 1/2 pound broccoli florets, finely chopped
- 1 tbsp. butter
- 2 tbsp. onions, finely chopped
- 1 clove garlic, minced
- 1 cup milk
- 1 tbsp. flour
- 1/4 cup walnuts, chopped (optional)
- 1/2 cup low fat cheddar cheese, divided
- 2 tbsp. parmesan cheese, grated
- Salt to taste
- Pepper powder to taste

Method:

1. Place a skillet over medium heat. Add butter. When butter melts, add onions, garlic and mushrooms. Sauté until the onions are translucent.
2. Add salt, pepper and flour. Sauté until brown.
3. Gently pour milk. Stir constantly and bring to a boil. Simmer for a minute and remove from heat.
4. Add cheese and mix well.
5. Place rice in the cooker. Add water, broccoli, and cheese sauce. Mix.
6. Cover and cook on Low for 6 - 7 hours or until the rice is tender.
7. Uncover, sprinkle both cheddar cheese and Parmesan.
8. Cover and cook for one hour on Low.
9. Garnish with walnuts and serve.

Slow Cooked Creamed Corn

Ingredients

- 5/8 (16 ounce) package frozen corn kernels
- 1/4 cup butter
- 1/2 (8 ounce) package cream cheese
- 1/4 cup milk
- Salt, to taste
- 1 1/2 tsp. white sugar
- Freshly ground black pepper, to taste

Method:

1. Combine the cream cheese, milk and butter together in the bottom of a slow cooker.
2. Add in the sugar and mix well until the sugar has dissolved.
3. Add in the corn kernels and season to taste with the salt and pepper.
4. Cover the slow cooker and cook on the Low setting for 6 to 8 hour or on the High setting for 2 to 4 hours.
5. Serve warm with some fried chicken or roasted beef.
6. Enjoy!

Garlic Cauliflower Mashed Potatoes

Ingredients:

- 2 heads cauliflower, chopped into florets
- 8-10 large cloves garlic, peeled
- Salt to taste
- Pepper powder to taste
- 2 bay leaves
- 6 cups water
- A little milk if required
- 2 tbsp. butter

Method:

1. Add cauliflower, water, garlic, salt and bay leaves to the slow cooker. Mix well, cover and cook on Low for 4-6 hours.
2. Discard the bay leaves and excess moisture in the pot. Add butter. Mash the cauliflower with a potato masher or if you like a creamier consistency, blend with a stick blender.
3. Add a tbsp. or more of milk if it is too dry. Add pepper powder and more salt if necessary.
4. Serve with green onions.

Vegetarian Gumbo

Ingredients:

- 1/2 a 15 ounces can kidney beans, rinsed, drained
- 1/2 a 14.5 ounce can diced tomatoes
- 1 medium onion, chopped
- 1/2 a small zucchini, cut into thick half circles
- 1 stalk celery, chopped
- 1 small green bell pepper, chopped
- 4 ounces mushrooms, quartered
- 1/2 cup frozen sliced okra
- 2 cloves garlic, minced
- 1 tbsp. olive oil
- 1 tbsp. all-purpose flour
- 2 tsp. Cajun seasoning
- 1 tbsp. vegan Worcestershire sauce
- 1 bay leaf
- 1 cup vegetable broth
- Salt to taste
- Pepper powder to taste
- A dash of hot sauce to serve
- Hot cooked rice to serve

Method:

1. Place a skillet over medium heat. Add 1/2-tbsp oil. When oil is heated, add onion, bell pepper, celery and garlic and sauté until onions are translucent. Transfer into a slow cooker.
2. Place the skillet back on heat and add remaining oil. When oil is heated, add flour and stir constantly until it turns light brown.
3. Add broth stirring constantly and bring to a boil. Transfer into the cooker.
4. Add rest of the ingredients except rice and hot sauce.
5. Cover and cook on Low for 6 - 8 hours.
6. When done, discard the bay leaf. Taste and adjust the seasonings if necessary.
7. Serve over hot cooked rice. Drizzle a bit of hot sauce on top.

Chickpeas and Vegetable Curry

Ingredients:

- ½ tbsp. vegetable oil
- 1 medium brown onion, chopped
- 1 clove garlic, crushed
- 1 tbsp. curry powder
- 1 ½ tsp. cumin, powdered
- 14 oz. canned tomatoes, diced
- 1 tbsp. lemon juice (you can add more for a tangy taste)
- 5 ¼ oz. canned chickpeas, strained, rinsed
- 2 ½ oz. orange sweet potato, peeled, diced
- 1 medium carrot, peeled, diced
- 1 small red bell pepper, diced
- 4 ½ oz. cauliflower, broken into florets
- 1 ¾ oz. button mushrooms, halved
- 2 small yellow summer squash, halved
- 4 ½ oz. broccoli, broken into florets
- Steamed Jasmine Rice to serve
- Plain yogurt to serve

Method:

1. Place a saucepan over medium heat. Add oil in the saucepan. When thoroughly heated, add onion. Sauté for a couple of minutes.
2. Add garlic, curry powder and cumin powder. Sauté for about a minute.
3. Add tomatoes. Lower the heat and simmer for 3 minutes or until the sauce has become thick.
4. Add ¼ cup cold water. Add lemon juice, chickpeas and vegetables. Increase the heat. When it starts boiling, turn off the heat.
5. Transfer the contents into the slow cooker.
6. Cover. Set on High and cook for 4 hours or Low for 6 hours.
7. Add salt and pepper.
8. To serve, pour the curry over rice. Serve along with yogurt.

Spinach with Sweet Potatoes

Ingredients:

- 1 pound sweet potatoes, scrubbed
- 1 medium onion, chopped
- 1 pound spinach, rinsed, chopped
- 2 tomatoes, pureed
- 1 tsp. whole cumin
- 1 inch piece cinnamon
- 4 whole cloves
- 1/2 tsp. turmeric powder
- 1/2 tsp. chili powder
- 1/2 tsp. ground coriander
- 1/2 tsp. ground cumin
- 2 tsp. oil
- 1 tsp. salt or to taste
- 1/2 cup water

Method:

1. Place a nonstick pan over medium heat. Add oil. When oil is heated, add cumin, cinnamon and cloves. When cinnamon crackles, add onions and sauté until translucent.
2. Add turmeric, coriander and cumin powders and sauté for a few seconds until fragrant.
3. Transfer into the slow cooker. Add rest of the ingredients and stir.
4. Cover and set the cooker on High for 3 hours.
5. If possible, stir every hour. If there is too much moisture, then cook on high for a little more time to dry it

White Bean Cassoulet

Ingredients:

For Cassoulet:

- 1 can (15 ounces each) white beans of your choice, rinsed, drained
- 1/2 a 15 ounces can diced tomatoes
- 2 leeks, white parts only, sliced
- 1 stalk celery, chopped
- 1 large carrot, peeled, sliced
- 1 bay leaf
- 2 cloves garlic, minced
- 1 cup vegetable stock or water
- 1/2 tbsp. Italian seasoning
- Salt to taste
- Pepper powder to taste

For toasted bread crumbs:

- 1/2 cup coarse bread crumbs
- 1/2 tsp. garlic powder or minced garlic
- 2 tbsp. fresh parsley, chopped
- 1 tbsp. olive oil
- Zest of 1/2 a lemon

Method:

1. Place a skillet over medium heat. Add about a tbsp. stock. Add leeks and celery and sauté for 3-4 minutes.
2. Add carrots and cook for a couple of minutes more. Add garlic and sauté until fragrant. Transfer into the slow cooker.
3. Add rest of the ingredients for Cassoulet.
4. Cover and set the cooker on Low for 4 - 6 hours. If you like thicker gravy, remove some beans, mash it and add it back to the slow cooker.
5. Meanwhile, make the toasted breadcrumbs as follows: Mix together oil, breadcrumbs and garlic and spread on a baking sheet. Bake in a preheated oven at 350 degree F for about 10 minutes until lightly toasted.
6. Remove from the oven and cool. Add parsley and zest and mix.
7. To serve, place Cassoulet in bowls. Sprinkle toasted breadcrumbs over it and serve.

Chinese Tofu and Vegetables

Ingredients:

For vegetables:

- 2 pounds extra firm tofu, chop into 1/2 inch thick slices
- 5-6 stalks of broccoli (florets not needed), slice into 1/4 inch round thick slices
- 2 cans (8 ounce each) sliced water chestnuts
- 4 medium zucchini, cut into 1/2 inch cubes
- 1 medium red bell pepper, cut into 1 inch squares
- 1 medium green bell pepper, cut into 1 inch squares
- Cooking spray

For the sauce:

- 1 large onion, minced
- 6 cloves garlic, minced
- 2 tbsp. fresh ginger, minced
- 1/2 cup hoisin sauce
- 2 cups tomato sauce, unsalted
- 1 tsp. Worcestershire sauce
- 1/4 cup seasoned rice wine vinegar
- 2 tbsp. light soy sauce
- 4 tsp. molasses
- 1/4 cup water
- 2 tbsp. spicy brown mustard
- 1/2 tsp. crushed red pepper
- 1/2 tsp. five spice powder
- Black pepper powder to taste
- Salt to taste

Method:

1. Follow the manufacturer's instructions carefully and switch on the slow cooker.
2. Place the tofu slices on paper towels and press lightly to remove excess liquid from tofu. Once it is done chop into triangles.
3. Spray the inside of the slow cooker with cooking spray.
4. Place a nonstick skillet over medium heat. Spray with cooking spray. Add tofu slices in batches and cook on both the sides until brown. Transfer into the slow cooker.

5. To make the sauce: To the same skillet, spray a little more oil. Add onions, garlic and ginger. Sauté until onions are translucent.
6. Add rest of the ingredients, mix well and bring to a boil. Transfer the sauce into the slow cooker and pour over the tofu pieces.
   Cover and cook on Low for 5-6 hours or on High for 2 ½ - 3 hours. Add the vegetables into the pot. Mix well. Cover and cook on High for an hour. Serve over brown rice.

Cauliflower Bolognese with Zucchini Noodles

Ingredients:

For the Bolognese:

- 2 heads cauliflower, chopped into florets
- 1 large onion, chopped
- 4 cloves garlic, minced
- 2 cans (28 ounce each) diced tomatoes, unsalted
- 1/2 tsp. red pepper flakes
- 4 tsp. dried oregano
- 2 tsp. dried basil flakes
- Salt to taste
- Pepper powder to taste

For the noodles:

- 6 large zucchini

Method:

1. Add all the ingredients of the Bolognese to the slow cooker
2. Cover and cook on Low for 4 - 5 hours or on High for 3 1/2 hours.
3. Meanwhile, make noodles of zucchini using a spiralizer or a julienne peeler and set aside.
4. When done, mash the cauliflower with a potato masher.
5. If you like your noodles hot, then spray a nonstick skillet with cooking spray and zucchini noodles and heat thoroughly otherwise, enjoy it raw and crunchy.
6. Place the zucchini noodles in large individual serving bowls. Place the Bolognese over it and serve.

Chapter 13: Slow Cooker Dessert Recipes

Tapioca Pudding

Ingredients:

- 2 cups whole milk
- 5 tbsp. white sugar or as per taste for sweetness
- 1 tsp. vanilla extract
- 1/4 tsp. salt
- 1/4 cup small tapioca pearls
- 2 egg yolks

Method:

1. Add milk, sugar, vanilla extract, salt and tapioca pearls to the slow cooker.
2. Stir well until the sugar is completely dissolved.
3. Cover and cook on High or on Low for 2 hours or on Low and cook for 4 hours. Stir occasionally. Switch off the cooker.
4. Whisk the yolks well.
5. Add about 1 tbsp. of the hot pudding into the egg yolks. Mix thoroughly.
6. Repeat the process of adding the hot pudding mix to the egg yolks until all the pudding is added.
7. Transfer the contents back to the pot.
8. Uncover and look on Low for about 5 minutes. Whisk constantly until the pudding is thickened.
9. Cover and cook on High for 30 minutes or Low and cook for 1 hour.
10. Top with berries or fruit and serve.

Carrot Cake with Cream Cheese

Ingredients:

- 1 ½ cups of almond flour
- ½ cup of shredded coconut
- ¾ cup of natural sweetener
- ½ cup of chopped walnuts
- 2 tsp of baking powder
- ¼ cup of whey protein powder (unflavored)
- 1 tsp of ground cinnamon
- ¼ tsp of salt
- ¼ tsp of ground cloves
- 2 cups of grated carrots
- ¼ cup of coconut oil, melted
- 4 large eggs
- 3 tbsp. of almond milk
- ½ tsp of vanilla extract
- 6 oz. of cream cheese, softened
- ¾ tsp of vanilla extract
- ½ cup of powdered natural sweetener
- ½ cup of heavy cream

Method:

1. Grease the sides of the slow cooker then line it with parchment paper.
2. In a mixing bowl, whisk the natural sweetener, almond flour, chopped walnuts, shredded coconut, baking powder, whey protein powder, cloves, cinnamon and salt together until properly combined.
3. Add in the eggs, carrots, almond milk, coconut oil and vanilla extract then stir until well incorporated.
4. Pour the batter into the slow cooker and cook for 3 ½ hours on low settings. Once done, let it cool completely before transferring on a serving platter.
5. To make the cream cheese frosting, beat the cream cheese together with the powdered natural sweetener until it forms a smooth mixture. Add in the vanilla extract and heavy cream and beat until properly combined. Spread the mixture over the cooled cake.

Tropical Ice Cream

Ingredients

- 2 bananas, cut into large chunks and frozen
- 1 cup mango chunks, frozen
- 2 cups watermelon, diced and frozen
- 1/2 cup almonds, silvered (optional)
- 1/2 cup strawberries, frozen
- 2 tsp. hemp seeds, or to taste (optional)

Method:

1. Place the frozen banana chunks, frozen mango chunks, frozen watermelon chunks and frozen strawberries in the jar of the blender. Blend until smooth.
2. If you are using hemp seeds; add them to the blender and blend until well mixed.
3. Pour the prepared ice cream into a freezer safe bowl. Add in the slivered almonds and mix by hand.
4. Scoop with a scooper dipped in warm water and serve immediately or freeze until ready to eat.
5. Enjoy!

Chocolate Pudding Cake

Ingredients:

- 3/4 cup cocoa
- 2 cups all-purpose flour
- 4 tsp. baking powder
- 2 tsp. vanilla extract
- 1/2 tsp. salt
- 4 tbsp. vegetable oil
- 1 cup sugar
- 1 1/2 cups brown sugar
- 3 cups hot water
- 1 cup milk
- Whipped cream to serve (optional)
- Cooking spray

Method:

1. Mix together in a bowl, sugar, 1/4-cup cocoa, baking powder and salt.
2. Pour milk, oil and vanilla and whisk well until smooth.
3. Transfer the batter into a greased slow cooker.
4. Mix together brown sugar and remaining cocoa and sprinkle over the batter in the cooker.
5. Pour hot water but do not mix the contents.
6. Cover and set the cooker on High for 2 hours. After about 2 hours, a toothpick when inserted at the center of the cake should come out clean.
7. When done, uncover and let it remain the cooker for at least 30 minutes.
8. Slice and serve with whipped cream if desired.

Caramel Poached Pears

Ingredients:

- 2 cups dark brown sugar
- 3 tbsp. unsalted butter, chopped into small pieces
- 8 bosc pears, peeled, cored, halved
- 2 tsp. ground ginger

Method:

1. Add brown sugar, ginger and butter to the slow cooker and mix well.
2. Add pears and toss well so as to coat the pears. Place the pears with its cut side on the bottom of the cooker.
3. Cover and cook on Low for 4 hours or on High for about 2 hours or the pears are tender.
4. Place a pear in individual bowl. Spoon the caramel sauce over it and serve.

Flan

Ingredients:

- 10 eggs
- 2 cups heavy cream
- 2 cups water
- 10 packets sugar substitute or to taste
- 2 tsp. almond extract
- ¼ tsp. cinnamon powder
- Cooking spray

Method:

1. Whisk together all the ingredients except the cinnamon powder.
2. Grease a baking dish that fits well into the slow cooker. Place it on the metal rack of the cooker.
3. Pour the whisked mixture into the baking dish. Sprinkle cinnamon powder. Cover the dish with aluminum foil.
4. Cover and cook on low for 6-7 hours or high for 2 hours or until set.
5. Can be served warm or chilled.

Apple Crisp

Ingredients:

- 2 cups flour
- 1 cup light brown sugar
- 1 cup white sugar or to taste
- 2 tsp. cinnamon, powdered
- ½ tsp. nutmeg, powdered
- 2 pinch salt
- 1 cup butter, cut into pieces
- 2 cups walnuts, chopped
- 1/3 cup white sugar, or to taste
- 2 tbsp. cornstarch
- 1/2 tsp. ground ginger
- 12 cups apples - peeled, cored and chopped
- 4 tbsp. lemon juice

Method:

1. In a bowl add flour, brown sugar, 1 cup white sugar, 1 tsp. cinnamon powder, nutmeg powder and salt. Mix well.
2. Add butter. Mix together using fork or by your hands until it forms a crumble.
3. Add walnuts and keep aside.
4. In another bowl add 1/3-cup sugar, cornstarch, ginger and 1 tsp. of cinnamon.
5. Place the apples in the slow cooker. Add the starch mixture
6. Add lemon juice and toss well.
7. Sprinkle the walnut and crumb mixture on the top.
8. Cover. Set on High and cook for 2 hours or Low and cook for 4 hours or until the apples are nice and tender.
9. During the last hour, partially uncover the cooker so that the topping hardens.
10. Serve warm with vanilla ice-cream

Carrot Pudding

Ingredients:

- 3 cups carrots, peeled, grated
- 3 cups low fat milk (1%)
- ¼ tsp. cardamom powder
- 1 tbsp. raisins
- 2 tbsp. almond, slivered
- Stevia drops to taste

Method:

1. Place the carrots and milk in the slow cooker.
2. Cover and cook on low for 4-5 hours.
3. Add raisins and stir. Cook for 30 minutes more.
4. If you like it thicker, then cook for some more time.
5. Add 1-½ tbsp. almonds, stevia drops, and cardamom. Mix well.
6. Serve warm sprinkled with the remaining almonds.

Pear Caramel Pudding

Ingredients:

- 1 cup all-purpose flour
- 1/3 cup granulated sugar
- 1 tbsp. flaxseed meal
- 1 tsp. baking powder
- A pinch salt
- 1/2 tsp. cinnamon powder
- 1/2 cup fat free milk
- 2 tbsp. canola oil
- 1/4 cup dried pears, snipped
- 1/2 cup water
- 1/2 cup pear nectar
- 6 tbsp. brown sugar
- 1 tbsp. butter
- Cooking spray

Method:

1. Mix together in a bowl flour, granulated sugar, flaxseed meal, and baking powder, cinnamon, and salt.
2. Add milk and oil. Mix well. Add pears.
3. Spray the inside of the slow cooker with cooking spray.
4. Pour the batter into the cooker.
5. Meanwhile mix together water, pear nectar, brown sugar, and butter in a saucepan. Heat it and bring to a boil. Boil for 2 minutes.
6. Pour this sugar solution over the batter in the cooker.
7. Cover and cook on Low for 3 – 31/2 hours.
8. When done, switch off the cooker. Uncover and let it remain in the cooker for about 45 minutes.
9. Divide into bowls and serve.

Cranberry Stuffed Apples

Ingredients:

- 6 medium apples
- 3 tbsp. walnuts, chopped
- 1/3 cup packed brown sugar
- 1/2 cup fresh or frozen cranberries, thawed, chopped
- 1/4 tsp. ground nutmeg
- 1/2 tsp. ground cinnamon
- Whipped cream to serve (optional)

Method:

1. Leave the bottom part of the apples intact and core the apples. Slowly scoop out some more apples from inside the apple.
2. Mix together rest of the ingredients and stuff inside the apple.
3. Place the apples in a slow cooker.
4. Cover and set the cooker on Low for 4-5 hours.
5. Serve with whipped cream if desired.

Conclusion

Despite— and in many cases because of— the many technological advances that work to make our lives easier and more fun, we seem to have less time than ever before. When we're not in the office, at school, or fitting in a little bit of time for hobbies, our minutes seem to be dominated by devices, whether we're checking e-mail, playing games, or streaming one television show after the next. Trying to create additional time for healthy, flavorful meals that don't create another problem— tons of leftovers and days upon days of eating the same meals— can feel impossible.

That's where slow cooking comes in. This old-school appliance, getting ever more modern and popular each year, doesn't judge you for where and how you want to spend your time. It simply accepts the burden of doing your cooking for you.

Slow Cookers focus mainly on cooking the food slowly over many hours while at the same time retaining the original taste. Slow Cookers work on two basic principles – using the heating units to cook the food and letting pressure developed between the ingredients and the lid to add more flavor to the food.

Slow Cookers can cook anything – many people believe that slow cookers can only cook certain kinds of food but that is totally false. From pork to lasagna – you can cook all kinds of food with the help of a slow cooker without compromising on the taste. The best part about cooking with Slow Cookers is the how your food is warm whenever you come home. After cooking the food, Slow Cookers switch to a warm setting which uses minimum heat to keep the food warm until it's time for serving.

Slow cooking is so much easier and healthier than cooking a microwave dinner or going to a drive-through for some fast food, and the food that comes out of this appliance is delicious, well flavored, complex, and interesting.

I hope that this cookbook taught you the value of slow cookers and you were able to make some delicious meals for your friends or family.

Made in the USA
Middletown, DE
11 December 2017